THE INDIAN QUESTION.

BY

FRANCIS A. WALKER,

LATE U. S. COMMISSIONER OF INDIAN AFFAIRS.

BOSTON:

JAMES R. OSGOOD AND COMPANY,

(LATE TICKNOR AND FIELDS, AND FIELDS, OSGOOD, & CO.)

1874.

BOSTON:
RAND, AVERY, & CO., STEREOTYPERS AND PRINTERS.

CONTENTS.

THE INDIAN QUESTION.*

On the 3d of March, 1871, Congress declared that "hereafter no Indian nation or tribe within the territory of the United States shall be acknowledged or recognized as an independent nation, tribe, or power, with whom the United States may contract by treaty."

Brave words these would have seemed to good William Penn, treating with the Lenni Lenape, under the elm at Kensington; or even to doughty Miles Standish, ready as that worthy ever was to march against the heathen who troubled his Israel. Heathen they were in the eyes of the good people of Plymouth Colony, but nations of heathen, without question, as truly as were the Amalekites, the Jebusites, or the Hittites to the infant colony at Shiloh. It would have been deemed the tallest kind of "tall talk," in the councils of Jamestown,

* From "The North American Review," April, 1873.

Providence, and Annapolis, to express disdain for the proffered hand of Indian friendship, or even to object to payment of some small tribute, in beads or powder, to these native lords of the continent. In 1637, when Capt. John Mason marched against Sassacus, at the head of ninety men, he had with him half the fighting force of the Connecticut Colony. In 1653 a wall was built across Manhattan Island to keep out the savages; though, when we say that the line of defence just covered the present course of Wall Street (which derives its name from that circumstance), our readers may not fail to wonder whether the savages were not the rather kept in by it. In 1675, when the New-England Colonies had grown comparatively strong, they mustered for their war against Philip one thousand men, of whom Massachusetts furnished five hundred and twenty-seven, Plymouth one hundred and fifty-eight, and Connecticut three hundred and fifteen.

To men peering out from block-houses, or crouching behind walls, awaiting the terrific yell of an Indian attack, it was not likely to occur that they might compromise their dignity by treating on equal terms with an enemy tenfold as numerous as themselves; nor were the statesmen of that early heroic age likely to give themselves trouble about the character and standing among the nations of the earth, of confederacies that could bring five thousand warriors into the field. And so the feeble colonies struggled on through those days of gloom and fear, deprecating the anger of the savages as they might, and circumventing their wiles when they could; played off one chieftain against another; made contribution of malice and powder to every intestine feud among the natives; bought off tribes, without much scruple as to the ultimate fulfilment of their bargains; postponed the evil day by every expedient, knowing that time was on their side: and when they had, in spite of all, to fight, fought as men who know that they will not themselves be spared, — planned ambuscades and massacres; fired Indian camps, and shot the inmates as they leaped from their blazing wigwams; studied and mastered all the arts of forest warfare; and beat the savages with their own weapons, as men of the higher race will always do when forced by circumstances to such a contest.

Nor during the early part of the eighteenth century, when all danger of a war of extermination had passed from the apprehension of the most timid, when the Colonies had become in a degree compacted, and the line of white occupation had been made continuous from Massachusetts to Georgia; nor later still, when the Colonies had become States, and the representatives of the new nation of the Western world were received in all the courts of Europe, — was the policy abandoned of treating with the Indian tribes as parties having equal powers of initiative, and equal rights in negotiation. In nearly four hundred treaties, confirmed by the Senate as are treaties with foreign powers, our government recognized Indian tribes as nations with whom the United States might contract without derogating from its sovereignty.

The treaties made with Indian tribes have, of course, been mainly treaties of cession. Most of our readers will be surprised to learn the extent of lands east of the Mississippi which are embraced in sales to the United States; being no less than the entire States of Ohio, Indiana, Illinois, Georgia, Florida, Alabama, and Mississippi, with considerable portions of Tennessee, Michigan, and Wisconsin. And these treaties were not a mere form to amuse and quiet savages, a half-compassionate, half-contemptuous humoring of unruly children. The

United States were not then grown so great that they could afford to value lightly the free relinquishment of the soil by the native owners of it. At the time most of the treaties with tribes east of the Mississippi were concluded, not only did the right remain in the Indians, but enough of power, to make it as much a diplomatic triumph to obtain a cession on favorable terms, as it would be to negotiate a successful treaty with one of the States of Central America to-day. The United States were clearly the stronger party in every such case; but the Indians were, in the great body of instances, still so formidable, that to wrest their lands from them by pure, brutal violence would have required an exertion of strength which the government was ill prepared to make. So that, while it is true that the Indians were generally made ready to negotiate by the use of military force and by the pressure of white settlements, it is not true that the considerations and privileges accorded them in these treaties were a gift out of good-nature.

So much for the power of the Indians when they made these treaties. Their right to their lands is quite as well established historically. In the early history of the Western world, the principle was fully recognized, that, while sovereignty rested, not with the Indians, but with the civilized power claiming by virtue of discovery, the Indians were the rightful occupants, with a just and perfect claim to retain possession and enjoy the use until they should be disposed voluntarily to part with it. Great Britain, Holland, France, and Spain, the four powers claiming sovereignty by virtue of discovery within the present territory of the United States, conceded no less than this to the natives; while France, in the cession of the province of Louisiana, expressly reserved the rights allowed the Indians by its own treaties and articles, "until, by mutual consent of the United States and the said tribes or nations, other suitable articles shall have been agreed upon."

"Such being the right of the Indians to the soil, the United States for more than eighty-five years pursued a uniform course of extinguishing the Indian title only with the consent of those Indian tribes which were recognized as having claim by reason of occupancy: such consent being expressed in treaties, to the formation of which both parties approached, as having equal rights of initiative, and equal rights in negotiation. These treaties were made from time to time (not less than 372 being embraced in the general statutes of the United States) as the pressure of white settlements, or the fear or the experience of Indian hostilities, made the demand for the removal of one tribe after another urgent or imperative. *Except only in the case of the Indians in Minnesota, after the outbreak of* 1862, *the United-States Government has never extinguished an Indian title as by right of conquest;* and in this latter case the government provided the Indians another reservation, besides giving them the proceeds of the sales of the lands vacated by them in Minnesota; so scrupulously, up to that time, had the right of the Indians to the soil been respected, at least in form. It is not to be denied that wrong was often done in fact to tribes in the negotiation of treaties of cession. The Indians were not infrequently overborne or deceived by the agents of the government in these transactions; sometimes unquestionably, powerful tribes were permitted to cede lands to which weaker tribes had a better claim: but, formally at least, the United States accepted the cession successively of all lands, to which Indian tribes could show color of title, which are embraced in the limits of any of the present States of the Union except California and Nevada." — *Report on Indian Affairs*, 1872, pp. 83, 84.

In 1871, however, the insolence of conscious strength, and the growing jealousy of the House of Representatives towards the prerogative — arrogated by the Senate — of determining, in connection with the executive, all questions of Indian right and title, and of committing the United States incidentally to pecuniary obligations limited only by its own discretion, for which the House should be bound to make provision without inquiry, led to the adoption, after several severe parliamentary struggles, of the declaration which stands at the head of this paper.

In abruptly terminating thus the long series of Indian treaties, and forever closing the only course of procedure known for the adjustment of difficulties, and even for the administration of ordinary business, with Indian tribes, Congress provided no substitute, and up to the present time has neglected to prescribe the methods by which, after the abrogation of the national character of the Indians, either their internal matters or their relations with the general government are to be regulated. The Indian-Intercourse Act of 1834, though still nominally in force, is so largely predicated upon the tribal constitution, and assumes so uniformly the national sufficiency of the tribe, that all the life and virtue are taken out of it by the Act of 1871 just cited; and the country is, in effect, left without rule or prescription for the government of Indian affairs. It is sufferance, not law, which enables the Indian Office to-day to administer its charge. While the Act of 1871 strikes down at a blow the hereditary authority of the chiefs, no legislation has invested Indian agents with magisterial powers, or provided for the assembling of the Indian *demos*. There is at this time no semblance of authority for the punishment of any crime which one Indian may commit against another, nor any mode of procedure, recognized by treaty or statute, for the regulation of matters between the government and the several tribes. So far as the law is concerned, complete anarchy exists in Indian affairs; and nothing but the singular homogeneity of Indian communities, and the almost unaccountable spontaneity and unanimity of public sentiment within them, has thus far prevented the attention of Congress and the country being called most painfully to the unpardonable negligence of the national legislature in failing to provide a substitute for the time-honored policy which was destroyed by the Act of 1871.

In treating the Indian question of the present day, the temptation is strongly felt, to dwell upon the history of Indian tribes, and upon the physical and moral characteristics of this singular race. Yet, if way be once given to this inclination, not only will the time and space necessary for a discussion of the present and the future of the Indian tribes be sacrificed, but the attention of the reader will be so overwhelmed with the multitude of names and incidents, that he will be embarrassed rather than assisted in his understanding of the subject to be treated. The value, for our purpose, of facts and incidents in Indian history is not at all according to their value historically or romantically. Indeed, such has been the fatality to the aborigines of contact with the whites, that it may almost be said, the importance to-day of tribes is inversely as their importance in the annals of the country. Among the greatest figures of the past are those of bands and confederacies that have utterly disappeared from the continent, happy that their long, savage independence, and their brief, fierce resistance to the encroachments of the pale-face, were not to be succeeded by a dreary period of submission, humiliation, and dependence. Other tribes, that but a few generations ago shook the infant colonies with terror, or even dared to stand across the path of the Republic, and for a time flung a shadow as of eclipse over its destiny, are now represented upon the annuity or feeding-lists of the United States by a few score of diseased wretches, who hang about the settlements, begging and stealing where they can, and quarrelling like dogs over the entrails of the beeves that are slaughtered for them. Still other tribes, once warlike and powerful, have, by a fortunate turn of character and circumstance, become so rich and respectable as not only to deprive them of all romantic interest, but practically to take them out of the scope of the Indian question. Other tribes, still having among them men whose grandfathers besieged Detroit under Pontiac, are now resolved into citizens of the United States, eligible for the chief-justiceship or the presidency.

Such considerations as we have here briefly sketched suffice to show the inexpediency of entering upon Indian history, *qua* history, as an introduction to the discussion of the Indian problems of to-day. Equally obdurate must one be to the seductions of Indian ethnology, except so far only as it may simplify the classification of the present Indian population to refer tribes and bands to recognized groups or families, for the better or briefer characterization of their qualities and affinities.

Even stronger yet is the temptation to enter upon the analysis and portraiture of the original and native character of the North-American Indian. Voluptuary and stoic; swept by gusts of fury too terrible to be witnessed, yet imperturbable

bable beyond all men, under the ordinary excitements and accidents of life; garrulous, yet impenetrable; curious, yet himself reserved, proud and mean alike beyond compare; superior to torture and the presence of certain death, yet, by the standards of all other peoples, a coward in battle; capable of magnanimous actions which, when uncovered of all romance, are worthy of the best days of Roman virtue, yet more cunning, false, and cruel than the Bengalee,—this copper-colored sphinx, this riddle unread of men, equally fascinates and foils the inquirer.

This, however, is the Indian of history. The Indian for whom the government is called to provide subsistence and instruction presents no such psychological difficulties. Curious compound and strange self-contradiction as the red man is in his native character, in his traditional pursuits, and amid the surroundings of his own wild life; yet when broken down by the military power of the whites, thrown out of his familiar relations, his stupendous conceit with its glamour of savage pomp and glory rudely dispelled, his occupation gone, himself a beggar, the red man becomes the most commonplace person imaginable, of very simple nature, limited aspirations, and enormous appetites.

The Indian question naturally divides itself into two: What shall be done with the Indian as an obstacle to the national progress? What shall be done with him when, and so far as, he ceases to oppose or obstruct the extension of railways and settlements? It is because these two parts of the question have not been separately regarded that so much confusion has been introduced into the discussion of Indian affairs. Widely diverse, for example, as are the criticisms popularly expressed on what is known as the "Indian policy" of Pres. Grant's administration, the writer can confidently affirm, as the result of hundreds of interviews, formal and informal, stated and casual, friendly and the reverse, with men from every section of the country, of both parties, and of all professions, that he believes there is no political subject mooted to-day on which there are so slight differences of real opinion, or, indeed, such general consent when men will once come to terms with each other, and begin to talk about the same thing. He has never known a man, even from the Territories or the border States, make objection, on a candid statement, to the intentions and purposes of that administration towards the Indians, unless it were some man peculiarly vulgar and brutal, — such a one, for instance, as, if a Southerner, would give his time and breath to indiscriminate abuse of the negroes. Instead of there being two parties on this subject, there is, therefore, if the observations of the writer have been well made, no reason to suppose that any considerable division of opinion or feeling exists respecting the duty of the government, at the present moment, by the aborigines of the country.

Take the public sentiment of Arizona, for example. It is the almost universal belief throughout the country, that the people of this Territory have a deadly hostility to the Indians, and meditate nothing but mischief towards them; and it certainly must be admitted that press and people alike indulge in expressions which fairly bear that construction, and are quite enough to create an impression that the citizens of the Territory hate an Indian as an Indian, and have no humane sentiments whatever towards the race. And yet the writer would as soon leave the question, whether the government should render some kindly service to the Papagoes or to the Pimas and Maricopas, in the way of assisting them to self-maintenance, or of providing instruction in letters or in the mechanic arts, to the general voice of the people of Arizona, as to any missionary association in New York or Boston the coming May. When the press of Arizona cry out against the Indian policy of the government, and denounce Eastern philanthropy, they have in mind the warlike and depredating bands; and they are exasperated by what they deem, perhaps unreasonably but not unnaturally, the weakness and indecision of the executive in failing to properly protect the frontier. Indians to them mean Apaches; and their violence on the Indian question arises from the belief that the administration of Indian affairs has been committed to sentimentalists, who have no appreciation of the terrible stress which those Indian outrages bring upon the remote settlements. But were the question one of helping, in a practical fashion suited to the habits and views of life of a border community, a tribe of Indians who are peaceful, and in a poor way helpful, there is no reason to suppose that the inhabitants of Tucson or Prescott would be behind an Eastern congregation in readiness for the work. And this impression the writer derives, not alone from the amiable and cultivated gentleman who represents that Territory in Congress, but from contact and correspondence with many influential and representative citizens of Arizona, and from a study of the very journals that so teem with denunciations of the Indian policy of the government.*

On the other hand, in our prosperous and well-ordered communities at the East, a gentleman of leisure and of native benevolence, whose ears

* The writer does not intend to say that the citizens of the border States are always just or reasonable in their disposition towards the Indians. It cannot be denied, that, in the exasperation of conflict, they often commit atrocities rivalling those of the savages; that, moreover, under the smart of wrong, they are very often indiscriminating in their revenge, and do cruel injustice to peaceful bands; and that, with the recklessness characteristic of border talk, they indulge to a vast extent in denunciations of horrible sound. To this is added, that in such communities are found more than the usual number of persons of a natural malignity of disposition, often refugees from criminal justice, who delight in committing outrages upon the exposed and helpless members of an inferior race. The opinion which the writer has given above is entirely consistent with the present admissions. The animosities felt and expressed are not towards the Indians as Indians, but arise out of the sense of injuries suffered, and the apprehension of further suffering. Were the Indians once rendered, by the extension and strengthening of our settlements, powerless for harm, the easy tolerance, the rough good-nature, and the quick condonement of wrong, which characterize pioneer communities, would speedily reconcile the whites to their presence, and establish relations not wholly unworthy of both parties.

have never rung with the war-whoop, whose eyes have never witnessed the horrid atrocities of Indian warfare, and who is only disturbed in his pleasing reveries by the occasional tramp of the policeman about his house, is apt to dwell exclusively upon the other side of the Indian question. To such a man, as he recalls the undoubted wrongs done the Indian in the past, as he contemplates the fate of a race whose heroic and romantic qualities have been greatly exaggerated, or as he listens to the flattering tale of a missionary returned from some peaceful and half-civilized tribe, it is very pleasant to think that the original owners of the soil are to be protected by the government, saved to humanity, educated in the useful arts, and elevated to a Christian civilization. On such a man accounts of Indian outrages make little impression. He regards them as the invention of pioneer malice, or easily disposes of them by a mental reference to the crimes perpetrated in his own town or city. He is, perhaps, so ignorant of Indian matters as to think that all the Indians of the country form one homogeneous community, and cannot understand how it should be, that, while Cherokees are supporting churches and colleges and orphan asylums at home, and sending their sons to receive classical and professional education in the best schools of the East, Kiowas should roast their prisoners alive, and brain the babe before the eyes of its mother. Is it a matter of wonder, that men who are contemplating things so different as are the Eastern philanthropist and the Western settler, when Indians are spoken of, should imagine that they disagree as to the policy of the government, and come to entertain contempt or repugnance for each other, while, in fact, on an honest statement of a given case, neither would dissent in the slightest degree from the views of the other? If there is, then, such a liability to confusion and misapprehension in the discussion of the Indian question, we may be allowed to insist strongly upon the necessity of the distinction indicated.

The actually or potentially hostile tribes of the United States number, on a rough computation suited to the rudeness of the definition, sixty-four thousand. It is these only which we have to treat under the first division of our question, — What shall be done with the Indian as an obstacle to the national progress? This number of sixty-four thousand is made up as follows: The actually depredating bands, North-west and South-west, probably have not exceeded, during the past year, seven thousand, mainly Kiowas, Comanches, and Apaches. The tribes with which these bands are directly and intimately connected contain about twenty thousand, including the marauders. There are further included in this calculation tribes and bands, numbering in the aggregate about forty-four thousand, which are now generally at peace.

It will be seen that the number which we have taken for the potentially hostile Indians is many times greater than the number of the actually hostile. Yet, on the other hand, we have not intended to embrace all those tribes which might be exasperated to the point of resistance by a reckless disregard of treaties on the part of the government, or by a series of wanton acts of abuse on the part of white settlers. There is a line beyond which no man or people may safely be pressed; and there are few bands of Indians, East or West, however contemptible in numbers or character, which, if wronged and trampled on, might not in their indignant despair teach their oppressors a lesson at which the world would shudder. We are contemplating no such possibilities. We are assuming that the government will, as it has generally done in the past, respect treaty obligations, and that the intercourse of the Indians with their white neighbors will be marked by only such sporadic acts of individual wrong as are in the nature of the case.

The tribes to which we refer as potentially hostile are, first, those now in immediate contact with the whites, whose claims to territory are so far disregarded, either by the action of the government or by the unauthorized intrusion of pioneers and prospectors; or whose means of subsistence are so far impaired or threatened by the extension of railways and settlements, — that hostilities are only prevented by the bounty of the government in feeding the members of such tribes in whole or in part, by liberal presents of trinkets and useful goods, by the exercise of especial watchfulness in avoiding occasions of dispute and points of collision, and finally by a willingness on the part of the government to overlook offences and even to tolerate a degree of insolence, rather than allow a breach of the peace: second, those tribes not now to any great extent in contact with the whites, and exhibiting no desire to go out of their way to make trouble, but of which the same must, in the inevitable course of the national progress, in a few years become true as of the tribes embraced under the first class.

But these classes, as we have thus described them, are yet far too numerous for the facts of the case. We must still further reduce them by excluding all such tribes as, from location, from traditional friendship for the whites, or from weakness of character, are unlikely, in any event reasonably to be contemplated, to become involved in hostilities.

Among the Indians, who, by the force of their location and surroundings, are rendered powerless for armed resistance, are not a few of the Indians of Minnesota, and even some in Wisconsin, who have no love for the whites, and would make exceedingly bad neighbors to frontier settlements, but who, encircled as they are by powerful communities, submit sullenly to their condition. The same may be said of many bands in Kansas, Nebraska, and on the Pacific coast. These are Indians who have been overtaken, surrounded, and disarmed by the progress of population, but, either through the neglect of the government or by the failure of the usual agencies of instruction and industrial assistance, have remained barbarous, and, as their natural means of subsistence grow scantier, are becoming every year more miserable.

There is another and much larger class of Indians from whom no organized violence is to be expected in the course of the complete settlement of the country, not because they are rendered helpless by the force of their location, nor because they have any traditional friendship for the whites, nor because they do not experience suffering enough to impel a warlike people to a struggle for life, but because they are not fighting Indians. Actual outrage might drive some of these tribes to resistance; but, under the slow wasting-away of their means of subsistence, and the gradual pressure of the settlements, they are, and are likely to remain, wholly passive, accepting their fate, and sinking to the lowest point of human misery without a single heroic effort. Some of these tribes have been "put upon" by their more warlike neighbors through many generations, driven from their original hunting-grounds, and harassed even in the mountains where they have taken refuge, until their spirit has been utterly crushed, and they have become as submissive as the Southern negroes. This is true of large numbers of the Indians of Colorado, Utah, Nevada, and Southern

California. They have neither the individual courage nor the instinct of confederation entitling them to be reckoned among the potentially hostile tribes.

Still, again, we count out several powerful tribes, able to bring five hundred or a thousand warriors each into the field, which, by reason of traditional friendship and their frequent alliance with our troops in campaigns against hostile Indians, are sure to remain the friends of the government under any tolerable treatment. Indeed, neglect and abuse seem insufficient to alienate these allies. Their faith once pledged, and friendship cemented by sacrifices and sufferings, they cling to the fortunes of the whites with romantic fidelity. Such are the Arickarees,* Mandans, and Gros Ventres

* The relations of the Arickarees — or, as they are commonly called, even in official reports, the 'Rees — to the government, form one of the most instructive chapters of Indian history. In 1838 the agent for the Upper Missouri Indian agency, in his annual report to the Department of Indian Affairs, used the following language in respect to this tribe: —

"The Riccaras have long been notorious for their treachery and barbarity, and, within my own recollection, have murdered and pillaged more of our citizens than all the other tribes between the western borders of Missouri and the heads of the Columbia River." — *Report on Indian Affairs*, 1838–9, p. 65.

This is language which one might expect from the agent of

of the Upper Missouri; such the Pawnees of Kansas; such the Flatheads, Kootenays, and Pend d'Oreilles, whose boast is that their tribes never killed a white man; such, in a degree, the Crows of Montana. These tribes, and others of less consequence, are not only sure, in the event of kindly treatment by the government, to remain its fast friends, but they may be relied upon in the future, as in the past, to do much to check the audacity of their hostile neighbors, and, in the last resort, to furnish re-enforcements of the most effec-

some exceptionally troublesome band of Sioux. But, to the contrary, in another portion of his report (*Ib.* p. 64) the same agent says, "No Indians ever manifested a greater degree of friendship for the whites in general, or more respect for our government, than the Sioux." This report was made thirty-four years ago, the limit of one human generation. To-day the Sioux are among the most dangerous and troublesome Indians on the hands of the government, while the Arickarees are our fast friends and allies. Lieut.-Gen. Sheridan, in 1871, writing of these Indians, now located at Fort Berthold, says, "They have always been civil and well disposed, and have been repaid by the government with neglect and starvation. Of all Indians in the country, they were the best entitled to be looked after, and made happy and contented." Something, clearly, has made this difference; and an inquirer would doubtless find here an explanation of no small part of the difficulties which the United-States Government has experienced in dealing with the Indian tribes.

tive and economical sort to the troops operating against predatory bands.

Having excluded all tribes and bands of the character, or in the position, indicated under the three heads above, we make up the list of the potentially hostile Indians somewhat as follows: of the Sioux of Dakota,—tribes, bands, and parties, to the number of fifteen thousand; of the Indians of Montana,—Blackfeet, Bloods, and Piegans, Assiniboines and roving Sioux, to the number of twenty thousand; of the Indians in the extreme southwestern part of the Indian Territory and on the borders of Texas,—Kiowas, Comanches, Cheyennes, and Arapahoes, to the number of seven thousand; of the Indians of Arizona,—Apaches of several tribes, to the number of nine thousand; of the mountain Indians of Colorado, Utah, and Nevada, to the number of five thousand; of the Indians of New Mexico, to the number of two thousand; and of the Indians in Oregon and Washington Territory, to the number of six thousand. The sixty-four thousand Indians thus enumerated comprise substantially all the tribes and bands with which the government is obliged to contemplate the possibility of war. It is in the highest degree improbable, however, that the United

States would, even in the event of what might properly be called a general Indian war, be called on to fight more than one-half of these Indians at any one time; while, with a reasonable policy of concession, the number of actually hostile and depredating bands may be steadily reduced, and the whole body of dangerous Indians held in check until the advance of population shall render them incapable of mischief. The measures by which this is to be effected must be considered candidly, in the light of the alternative presented, and not as if they were proposed as measures wholly agreeable to the tastes or the temper of those who are called to administer Indian affairs.

That we may obtain a true impression of one of the conditions on which peace is maintained with certain Indian tribes, let us take a leaf out of the official record of the dealings of the government with the Sioux during the past year. Early in 1872 an unusually large number of Indians were assembled at the Red Cloud agency, near Fort Laramie in Wyoming. By far the greater part were *habitués* of this or some other Sioux agency; but among them were many Northern Indians, who were for the first time the guests of the government, and who, not having become accustomed to eat the bread of dependence, were much more intractable and insolent than the others. The presence of these Indians produced great turmoil at the agency, and considerable apprehension on the part of the agent. Nothing in the nature of an outbreak occurred, however: the strangers gradually went away to their summer hunt on the Powder River; and the agency was brought back to its usual condition. But, while this was being effected, a ranchman named Powell, who had a large drove of cattle near Fort Laramie, was robbed and murdered. The bloody details were soon known; for Indians are such inveterate gossips that they can keep no secret, however dangerous disclosure may be to them. The murderers were Northern Indians, who had instantly left for their own country. At two successive councils, both the civil and the military authorities demanded the surrender of the guilty parties and the return of the stolen stock. The chiefs present and the great body of their followers most unmistakably disapproved and regretted the act, if for no better reason than because they apprehended the consequences; but they disclaimed any responsibility therefor, — the murderers not being of their own proper number, — pleaded their inability to arrest the fugitives with their bloody spoils, and, for the rest, did nothing. The government, for that matter, after much expostulation, did the same: troops were not marched northward to seize the murderers; the rations of the Sioux were not ordered to be stopped until satisfaction had been given; and the murder of Powell remains to-day unpunished by the government of the United States.

A second condition on which peace is maintained is the subsistence of certain tribes at the expense of the government, without reference to their ability or disposition to work. Every five or seven days, twenty thousand Sioux, big and little, assemble around the agencies for the distribution of food. Soldiers' rations are dealt out: flour by the hundred sacks is delivered to them; beeves by the score are turned loose to be shot down and eaten up in savage fashion. The expense of this service is a million five hundred thousand dollars a year, — one-seventh the total cost of poor-support in the United States. About one million more is expended for the total or partial subsistence of other tribes, especially in the South-west. Coincidently with this, occasions for increased expenditure have arisen in connection with tribes not upon the feeding-list; so that the average cost of the Indian service has gone up from four millions in 1866, 1867, and 1868, to seven millions at the present time. It should be remarked, however, that it is only the increase which measures the cost of the "peace policy," so called, more than one-half of the four millions of expenditure in the former period being the lawful due of the Indians under treaty stipulations, in consideration for the cession of lands; and the remainder covering the general expenses of the service. The following table exhibits the expenditures of the government on account of the Indian service for the twelve years 1861 to 1872: —

Year.	Expenditures on Indian Account.	Year.	Expenditures on Indian Account.
1861	$2,865,481.17	1867	$4,642,531,77
1862	2,327,948.37	1868	4,100,682.32
1863	3,152,032.70	1869	7,042,923.06
1864	2,629,975.97	1870	3,407,938.15
1865	5,059,360.71	1871	7,426,997.44
1866	3,295,729.32	1872	7,061,728.82

Now, it must honestly be confessed, that the United-States Government, in such dealings with Indian tribes as have been recited, does not act a very handsome part. To pay blackmail to insolent savages (for that is simply what it amounts to); to feed forty or fifty thousand people who make no pretence of doing any thing for themselves, and who appear to think that they are conferring a distinguishing honor upon the government by accepting its bounty; to allow the murder of an American citizen, of whatever character or degree, to go unpunished, — these are not things pleasant to contemplate. It may be a duty to administer Indian affairs in this way; but it must be a duty far more disagreeable to any man of spirit than would be a call to take part in the punishment of the savages, at no more than the personal risk usually incident to a campaign. And yet, in the face of all this, we do not hesitate to say that the general course of the government in such dealings as have been described above is expedient and humane, just and honorable. This is a proposition, which, in the view of such admissions as have been made, may seem to impose a formidable burden of proof; yet is it not only consistent with the highest reason of the case, but susceptible of very simple and direct demonstration.

In the first place, it should be remarked that there can be no question of national dignity involved in the treatment of savages by a civilized power. The proudest Anglo-Saxon will climb a tree with a bear behind him, and deem not his honor, but his safety, compromised by the situation. With wild men, as with wild beasts, the question whether to fight, coax, or run, is a question merely of what is easiest or safest in the situation given. Points of dignity only arise between those who are, or assume to be, equals. Indeed, nothing is at times so contemptuous as compliance. It indicates not merely a consciousness of strength, but of strength so superior as to decline comparison or contest.

Grant that some petty Sioux chief believes that the government of the United States feeds him and his lazy followers out of fear, or out of respect for his greatness: what then? It will not be long before the agent of the government will be pointing out the particular row of potatoes which his majesty must hoe before his majesty can dine. The people of the United States surely are great enough, and sufficiently conscious of their greatness, to indulge a little longer the self-complacent fancies of those savage tribes, if by that means a desolating war may be avoided.

And in this we shall only do what other nations

have done, and esteemed themselves wise in doing. The Greeks and Romans, except in periods of ambitious frenzy, recognized the fruitlessness and folly of fighting absolute savages, and did not scruple, in the height of their conquering pride, to keep the peace with Scythians and Parthians as best they could. The English, the Dutch, the Spanish, the Portuguese, in their American colonies, only fought the natives when for their purposes they must, preserving the peace when they could by presents, and even by tribute. Statesmen who would have embroiled Europe on a question of dinner-etiquette have fully recognized the principle that there could be no issue of dignity between a civilized power and a band of irresponsible savages, and have submitted, without any feeling of degradation, to demands the most unreasonable, urged in terms the most insolent.

Nor is there any savor of treachery in the government thus biding its time. In this the government simply, from a wise consideration of the exposed situation of the settlements, refrains from the full exercise of the authority which it claims. It in no wise deceives the Indians, but only indulges their illusion till the time comes when the illusion must be broken. It watches the troubled sleep of the maniac, ready to restrain his violence if he wakes, yet mercifully willing that he should remain unconscious. And this forbearance of the government is not less kind to the aborigines than to those of our citizens who are building their homes within reach of the red man's hand. If the savages — Sioux, Kiowas, Cheyennes, Comanches, whom the United States are thus playing with — realized in any adequate measure what the next few years have in store for them, how completely they will be surrounded and disarmed, how certainly they will be forced to labor like squaws for their bread, how stringently the government will enforce its requirements when their power of resistance shall have departed; it is inconceivable but that, in their present temper, ignorant as they are of the real resources of the whites, and conscious that they can still bring eight thousand warriors into the field, they would precipitate a contest which, though it would involve untold misery to our border population, must inevitably end in their own destruction.

If, then, there is nothing inconsistent with national dignity or honor in thus temporizing with hostile savages, it certainly can be shown to be in a high degree compatible with the interests and the welfare of all the white communities which are, by their advanced position, placed at the mercy of the Indians. Thousands and even tens of thousands of our citizens are now living within reach of the first murderous outbreak of a general Indian war. Since 1868, when the trans-continental railroad was completed, population has found its way into regions to which the rate of progress previously maintained would not in fifty years have carried it,—into nooks and corners which five years ago were scarcely known to trappers and guides. Instead of exposing to Indian contact, as heretofore, a clearly defined frontier line, upon two or three faces, our settlements have penetrated the Western country in every direction and from every direction, creeping along the course of every stream, seeking out every habitable valley, following up every indication of gold among the ravines and mountains, clinging around the reservations of the most formidable tribes, and even making lodgement at a hundred points on lands secured by treaty to the Indians. Even where the limit of settlement in any direction has apparently, for the time, been reached, we learn of some solitary ranchman or miner who has made his home still farther down the valley or up the mountain, far beyond sight or call.

It is upon men thus exposed, without hope of escape or chance of resistance, that the first wrath of a general Indian war would break. No note of recall would avert their doom. Long before friendly runners could reach them, the war-whoop would be in their ears; and alone, unfriended, undefended, unaided, they would perish, as hundreds and thousands of our countrymen have perished, at the hands of the infuriated savages. But it is not alone the solitary ranchmen who would be swept away on the first onset of Indian attack. Scores of valleys up which population has been steadily creeping would be instantly abandoned; streams that now, from source to mouth, resound the stroke of the pioneer's axe, would be left desolate on the first rumor of war; a hundred outlying settlements would disappear in a night, as the tidings of outbreak and massacre were borne along by hurrying fugitives. As the blood retreats, on the signal of danger, from the extremities to the heart, so would population retire, terror-struck and precipitate, from the frontier on the first shock of war. Towns, even, would be abandoned; and the frightened inhabitants, men, women, and children, cumbered with household stuff and overdriven stock, would crowd within the shelter of garrisons hardly adequate for their defence.

There could be but one plea on which such considerations as these might be disregarded; and that would be the plea that such forbearance and indulgence on the part of the United States towards the savages only encouraged them to increased insolence and incited them to fresh outrages, rendering the situation less and less tolerable, and in the end involving greater sacrifice of life than would a prompt vindication of the authority of the goverment, once for all, however disastrous in the immediate result it might prove to existing settlements. If the policy of temporizing which has been described does indeed only serve at the last to aggravate the evil, and by a false appearance of peace to draw within the reach of Indian massacre larger numbers of whites, then it is plainly the duty of the government to recall, as far as may be, its citizens from the exposed frontier, and, at whatever expense of blood and treasure, make issue with the savages, and forever close the question by the complete conquest and reduction of all the hostile or dangerous tribes. But no assumption could be farther from the facts of the case than that the effect of lenity has been to increase the sum of Indian outrage. There is no *scintilla* of evidence to show that any savage tribe has been incited by the forbearance of the government to increased depredations. On the contrary, the history of the past three years has shown a steady decline in the number of robberies and murders reported on the frontier.

If a humane consideration of the exposed condition of our frontier settlements requires the continuance of the policy of buying off the hostile and dangerous tribes, it is also true that the argument from economy equally favors this action on the part of the government. Expensive as is the Indian service as at present conducted in the interest of peace, it costs far less than fighting. What would be the expense of a general Indian war, which should seek the complete subjugation of the tribes which we have described as potentially hostile, it is impossible to compute within a hundred millions of dollars; but it would undoubtedly reach an aggregate not much short of that of the year of largest preparations and largest operations during the rebellion. Does this seem extravagant, impossible? Words of truth and soberness on such a subject surely might be expected from a commission comprising such men as Gens. Sherman, Harney, Augur, and Terry of the regular army of the United States. Yet these officers united in a report rendered to the President on the 7th of January, 1868, in which they use the following language in reference to the "Chivvington massacre" and the Cheyenne war of 1864:—

> "No one will be astonished that a war ensued which cost the government thirty million dollars, and carried conflagration and death to the border settlements. During the spring and summer of 1865, no less than eight thousand troops were withdrawn from the effective force engaged in suppressing the Rebellion, to meet this Indian war. The result of the year's campaign satisfied all reasonable men that war with Indians was useless and expensive. Fifteen or twenty Indians had been killed at an expense of more than a million dollars apiece, while hundreds of our soldiers had lost their lives, many of our border settlers had been butchered, and their property destroyed."

This was the experience of the United States in a contest with an Indian tribe numbering perhaps four thousand men, women, and children, and able to bring into the field not one-fifth as many warriors as the Sioux bands of to-day. Not to go back to wars waged with tribes now subjugated or extinct, were we to cast up the expenditures involved in the Sioux war of 1852–1854, the Cheyenne war of 1864 just referred to, the Navajo war, the second Sioux war in 1866, the second Cheyenne war in 1867, we should undoubtedly reach a total greatly exceeding one hundred millions of dollars. Yet these wars sought only the submission of individual tribes to single demands of the government, and effected, generally, something less than that. It has been shown that the actual expense of the so-called "peace policy" is measured by the increase of the average expenditures of the period 1869 to 1872 over the average expenditures of the period preceding, that increase being about three millions of dollars. This is the sum which is to be compared with the cost of a war which should seek to reduce all the Indian tribes of the continent to complete submission by force of arms, instead of awaiting their gradual, and in the main peaceful reduction through the advance of population and the extension of railways.

We have thus far treated the policy of the government towards the dangerous tribes as one not requiring the use of the military arm in any emergency short of an actual outbreak. We have done so, first, that we might encounter the full effect of the objections to the plan of concession and conciliation; and, secondly, because we hold it true, that, when the alternative is between allowing a considerable degree of insolence and outrage to go unpunished, and entailing upon the Territories a general Indian war, duty and interest require the government to go to the last point of endurance and forbearance with the savages. But this alternative is not always presented: it is often practicable to repress and punish violence, without exposing the settlements to the horrors of massacre. Whenever this can be done, it is scarcely necessary to say it should be done, and done effectually. The feature of the present Indian policy of the government which allows this to be done without incurring general Indian war is known as the reservation system, — a system shrewdly devised to meet the known weaknesses of the Indian character. By it extensive tracts have been set apart for the warlike tribes, within which they may pursue all their customs and habits of life, and indulge themselves in savagery, being also subsisted thereon to the extent of their actual necessities, but outside of which bands or parties are liable to be struck by the military at any time, without warning, and without any implied hostility to those members of the tribe who remain on their reservation, and deport themselves according to the conditions of the compact. The brilliant campaign of Gen. Crook in Arizona during the past season has been prosecuted with the most scrupulous observance of the reservation system, as marked out by the government, and accepted by the Indians themselves. Such a use of the military arm constitutes no abandonment of the "peace policy," and involves no disparagement of it. Military operations thus conducted are not in the nature of war, but of discipline, and are so recognized by the tribes whose marauding bands and parties are scourged back to the reservations by the troops.  The effect of all this is something more than negative. It does not merely serve to chastise offending individuals and parties without a breach of peace with the tribe; but it is made the means of impressing the less enterprising Indians with an increasing sense of the power of the government. It was not to be expected that the entire body of a warlike tribe would consent to be restrained in their Ishmaelitish proclivities without a struggle on the part of the more audacious to maintain their traditional freedom. The reservation system allows this issue to be fought out between our troops and the more daring of the savages, without involving in the contest tribes with which our army in its present numbers is wholly inadequate to cope.

Nor will the full effect of this consideration be appreciated if it be not borne in mind that the Indian is intensely susceptible to severe punishment. His own wars are so bloodless, his skirmishing tactics so cowardly and resultless, that the savage fighting of the whites, their eagerness for close quarters, and their deadly earnestness when engaged hand to hand, impress him with a strange terror. With him, as with all persons and peoples in whom the imagination is predominant, the effect of disaster is not measured by the actual loss and suffering entailed, but by the source, the shape, the suddenness, of it. Indeed, it is astonishing how completely the spirit of an Indian tribe may be broken by a catastrophe which does not necessarily impair its fighting power.

Nor even is it necessary that the Indian's

sense of justice should be met by the chastisement received. Undiscriminating in his own revenge, he does not look for nicely measured retribution on the part of his enemy. Hence it is that certain of the so-called — and sometimes properly so called — massacres perpetrated by the army, or by frontier militia, have had very different results from what would have been predicted by persons familiar only with habits of thought and feeling among our own people.* Injustice and cruelty exasperate men of our race; but the Indian is never other than cruel and unjust under resentment. Let him feel that he has been injured by a white man, and he will tomahawk the first white man he meets, without a thought whether his victim be guilty or innocent. Let him suffer at the hand of a member of a neighboring tribe, and he will lie all day in wait for another member

* To take one of the most recent examples: Col. Baker's attack upon a Piegan camp in 1869, even though it should be held to be justified on the ground of necessity, must be admitted to be utterly revolting in its conception and execution. Yet no merited chastisement ever wrought more instant and durable effects for good. The Piegans, who had been even more wild and intractable than the Sioux, have since that affair been orderly and peaceable. No complaints whatever are made of their conduct; and they are apparently as good Indians as can be found among the wholly uncivilized tribes.

of that tribe with just as much anticipation of gratified hate as if he awaited the footsteps of the wrong-doer. Nay, let him have a feud with one of his own blood, and he will devote the speechless babes of his enemy to his infernal malice. Here, undoubtedly, we find the explanation of the fact that massacres, damnable in plot and circumstance, have struck such deadly and lasting terror into tribes of savages; while, occurring between nations of whites, they would have kindled the flames of war to inextinguishable fury.

We have thus far treated the question, What shall be done with the Indian as an obstacle to the progress of railways and of settlements? — to the exclusion of the inquiry, What shall be done to promote his advancement in industry and the arts of life? — not merely because, for all those tribes and bands to which the first question applies (i. e. those which are potentially hostile, and towards which the government is, as we have attempted to show, bound in interest and humanity to exercise great forbearance till they shall cease to be formidable to the settlements and to the pioneers of settlement), that question is, in logical order, precedent to any discussion of methods to be taken to educate and civilize them; but also because it is in effect likewise precedent to any deliberate, comprehensive, and permanent adjustment of the difficulties experienced in treating the Indian tribes which are neither hostile in disposition nor formidable by reason of their situation or their numbers. So long as the attention of the executive department is occupied by efforts to preserve the peace; so long as Congress is asked yearly to appropriate three millions of dollars to feed and clothe insolent savages; so long as the public mind is exasperated by reports of Indian outrages occurring in any section of the country, — so long will it be vain to expect an adequate treatment of the question of Indian civilization.

It must not be understood that nothing is being done for the industrial and moral instruction of the peaceful and more advanced tribes* pending the reduction of their turbulent

* The Report on Indian Affairs for 1872 shows that, in addition to physicians, clerks, cooks, herders, teamsters, laborers, and interpreters, there are employed at all the agencies eighty-two teachers, eighty farmers, seventy-three blacksmiths, seventy-two carpenters, twenty-two millwrights and millers, seventeen engineers, eleven matrons of manual-labor schools, and three seamstresses. — *Report*, pp. 68-71.

brethren to terms; but the efforts and expenditures of the present time fall far short of the completeness and consistency necessary to constitute a system. Much that is doing is in compliance with treaty stipulations, and hence is well done, whether it have any practical result or not. Much, again, of what is doing, although so inadequate to the necessities of the situation as to yield no positive results, is preventing waste by keeping up established services and agencies, and, in a measure, preserving the character and habits of the Indians from further deterioration. Much, still, is in the way of experiment, from which may be derived many valuable principles and suggestions for the treatment of the Indian question on the larger scale which will be necessary in the future. Much, however, it must be confessed, is done out of an uneasy desire to do something for this unfortunate people, or in generous response to appeals from persons in official or private station who have chanced to become particularly interested in the welfare of individual tribes and bands, and thereafter fail not (small blame to them) to beset Congress and the departments for special consideration and provision for their *protégés*. It can scarcely need to be remarked, that these are not the ways to constitute a system.

It is a question not a little perplexing, What shall be done with the Indian when he shall be thrown helpless on our government and people? What *has* been done with tribes and bands which have reached this condition has been, as we have said, of every description; and the results have been not less various. We have had guardianship of the strictest sort. We have tried industrial experiments on more than one plan, and have attempted the thorough industrial education of Indian communities as a security for their social advancement. We have, on other occasions, let the Indian severely alone just so soon as it was ascertained that his power for harm had ceased, and have left him to find his place in the social and industrial scale; to become fisherman, lumberman, herdsman, menial, beggar, or thief, according to aptitude or accident, or the wants of the community at large. True it is that the modes adopted, in fact, in dealing with particular tribes, have generally been due to chance or to the caprices of administration; true, also, that the experiments which have been made do not reflect much credit on the sagacity of the superior race to which have been intrusted the destinies of the red man: but there has been a vast amount of good-nature and benevolent intention exhibited; the experiments have been in many directions, and have covered a large field; and while the results, in the manifest want of adaptation of means to ends, and of operations to material, cannot be deemed wholly conclusive of the philosophy of the situation, yet very much can be learned from them that bears upon the questions of the present day. As has been stated, the issues of the experiments tried have been of every kind. To assertions that the Indian cannot be civilized, can be opposed instances of Indian communities which have attained a very considerable degree of advancement in all the arts of life. To the more cautious assertion, that, while the tribes which subsist chiefly on a vegetable diet are susceptible of being tamed and improved, the meat-eating Indians, the buffalo and antelope hunters, are hopelessly intractable and savage, can be opposed instances of such tribes which, in an astonishingly short time, have been influenced to abandon the chase, to undertake agricultural pursuits, to labor with zeal and patience, to wear white man's clothes, send their children to school, attend church on Sunday, and choose their officers by ballot. To the assertion that the Indian, however seemingly reclaimed, and for a time regenerated, still retains his savage propensities and animal appetites, and will sooner or later relapse into barbarism, can be opposed instances of slow and steady growth in self-respect and self-control, extending over two generations, without an indication of the tendencies alleged. To assertions that the Indian cannot resist either physical or moral corruption by contact with the whites, that he inevitably becomes subject to the baser elements of civilized communities, that every form of infectious or contagious disease becomes doubly fatal to him, and that he learns all the vices but none of the virtues of society, can be opposed instances of tribes which have freely mingled with the whites without debasement, and have acquired the arts of civilized life with no undue proportion of its evils. To the assertion that the Indian must gradually decline in numbers and decay in strength, his life fading out before the intenser life which he encounters, can be offered instances of the steady increase in population of no small number of tribes and bands in immediate contact with settlements, and subject to the full force of white influence.

And yet it is undeniably true that many of the experiments have failed in a greater or less degree;

that in some cases the Indians most neglected have done better for themselves than those who have received the care and bounty of the government; that many tribes and bands which had apparently emerged from their barbarous condition have miserably fallen back into sloth and vicious habits; that the meat-eaters, who constitute the bulk of the tribes with which the latest advances of our settlements and railways have brought us in contact, are exceptionally wild and fierce; that the experiment of Indian civilization has far more chances of success when it is tried under conditions that allow of freedom from excitement, and thorough seclusion from foreign influences; and, finally, that Indian blood, thus far in the history of the country, has tended decidedly towards extinction.

The Board of Indian Commissioners, in their Report for 1872, make the statement that "nearly five-sixths of all the Indians of the United States and Territories are now either civilized or partially civilized." (Report, p. 3.) The Commissioner of Indian Affairs, in his report of the same date, places the number of reclaimed savages somewhat lower, dividing the three hundred thousand Indians within the limits of the United States as follows:

civilized, ninety-seven thousand; semi-civilized, one hundred and twenty-five thousand; wholly barbarous, seventy-eight thousand. He is, however, careful to explain that the division is made "according to a standard taken with reasonable reference to what might fairly be expected of a race with such antecedents and traditions." Perhaps, on a strict construction of the word "semi-civilized," the Indian Office might assent to take off twenty or thirty thousand from the number stated.

We all know what a savage Indian is. What is a civilized Indian?—what a semi-civilized Indian? To what degree of industry, frugality, and sobriety can the Indian be brought? How well does he repay efforts and expenditures for his enlightenment and his advancement in the arts of life? How far does he hold his own when once fairly started on his course by the bounty of the government or by philanthropic enterprise, instructed and equipped, with no obstacles in his way, and with no interruptions from without? What, in short, may we reasonably expect from this people? What have they done for themselves? or what has been done with them in the past? It is doubtful whether zeal or ignorance is more responsible for the confusion which exists in the public mind in respect to this entire matter of Indian civilization. The truth will be best shown by examples.

The Cherokees, who originally owned and occupied portions of the States of Georgia, Alabama, and Tennessee, have now a reservation of nearly four million acres in the tract known as the Indian Territory. They number about fifteen thousand, and are increasing. They have their own written language, their national constitution and laws, their churches, schools, and academies, their judges and courts. Their dwellings consist of five hundred frame and three thousand five hundred log houses. During the year 1872 they raised three million bushels of corn, besides large quantities of wheat, oats, and potatoes, their aggregate crops being greater than those of New Mexico and Utah combined. Their stock consists of sixteen thousand horses, seventy-five thousand neat-cattle, one hundred and sixty thousand hogs, and nine thousand sheep. It is needless, after such an enumeration of stock and crops, to say that they not only support themselves, but sell largely to neighboring communities less disposed to agriculture. The Cherokees have sixty schools in operation, with an aggregate attendance of two thousand one hundred and thirty-three scholars. Three of these schools are maintained for the instruction of their former negro slaves. All orphans of the tribe are supported at the public expense. The Cherokees are the creditors of the United States in the sum of a million seven hundred and sixteen thousand dollars, on account of lands and claims ceded and relinquished by them. The interest on this sum is annually paid by the treasurer of the United States to "the treasurer of the Cherokee nation," to be used under the direction of the national council for objects prescribed by law or treaty.

From the statements made above, all upon the authority of official reports, it will doubtless appear to every candid reader that the Cherokees are entitled to be ranked among civilized communities. Their condition is far better than that of the agricultural classes of England; and they are not inferior in intelligence or in the ability to assert their rights.

There are in the Indian Territory several other important tribes, and a number of small and broken bands, aggregating forty or forty-five thousand persons, who are in the same general condition as the Cherokees, and are equally —

though not, perhaps, in every case, with quite as much emphasis — entitled to be called civilized. Nor are the Indians of this class confined to the Indian Territory so called. They are found in Kansas and Nebraska, in New York, Michigan, Wisconsin, and Minnesota, and upon the Pacific coast. The ninety or one hundred thousand Indians thus characterized will bear comparison, on the three points of industry, frugality, and sobriety, with an equal population taken bodily out of any agricultural district in the Southern or border States. In general intelligence and political aptitude they are still necessarily below the lowest level of American citizenship, if we exclude the newly-enfranchised element and the poor white population of a few districts of the South.

It is just and proper to call an Indian semi-civilized, no matter how humble his attainments, when he has taken one distinct, unmistakable step from barbarism; since "it is the first step that costs."

The Sioux of the Lake Traverse agency in Dakota number about fifteen hundred, — to be exact, fourteen hundred and ninety-six. These were of the Indians of Minnesota, and escaped to the West after the massacre of 1862, though claiming to have been innocent of participation in it. They are genuine specimens of the Indian race in its pure form. They have within three or four years made considerable progress in agriculture. Nearly all the men have of choice adopted the dress of the whites. Great interest is manifested in the education of the children of the tribe: four schools are in operation, with an attendance of one hundred and twenty-three scholars; and two more schoolhouses are in course of erection. By the provisions of the treaty of 1867, only the sick, the infirm, aged widows, and orphans of tender years, are to be supported by the government. The number thus enrolled for subsistence during the past year was six hundred and sixty, made up as follows: ninety-two men, aged, infirm, blind, crippled, &c.; two hundred and sixty-four women of various conditions; one hundred and eighteen children under seven years; one hundred and eighty-six children between seven and sixteen years. The remainder of the tribe supported themselves fully by their own labor. The agent says, "It is highly gratifying to be able to report commendable progress in agriculture by these Sisseton and Wahpeton Sioux on this reservation, who, almost to a man, have become fully satisfied that they cannot any longer rely upon the chase, but must of necessity turn their attention to the cultivation of the soil and stock-growing, for the future, as the only reliable source of subsistence. Many of them have learned to work; and some of them have learned to love to work as well; and they evidently enjoy the labor of their hands."

Tribes which show a higher actual attainment might have been taken for illustration out of the semi-civilized list; but these have been chosen, first, because they are meat-eating Indians, and secondly, because the plan of partial support adopted with them is the one most likely to be applied to all the Sioux bands, as fast as the government shall find itself in a position peremptorily to control their actions and movements.

Again: we select the Pawnees, numbering twenty-four hundred and forty-seven, for illustration, for the reason that they have been long distinguished over all the plains for their warlike power and ferocity, yet, under the care and instruction of the government, have within three years made a great degree of progress in three most important respects, as follows: —

First, while the Pawnees, from their situation,

are still enabled and disposed to go upon the summer hunt, they are already engaged to a small extent, and with encouraging success, in the raising of vegetables and garden products, and even of corn and wheat. Two hundred and ten acres were planted by them last year in the several crops.

Second, while the chiefs and braves of the tribe still look to their traditional resource of hunting, the children of the tribe generally are being carefully instructed in letters and in labor. The day-schools and the manual-labor schools of the Pawnees have elicited the most enthusiastic praise from all persons, official or private, who have visited the reservation.

Third, — and this is a point to which we ask special attention, as indicating capabilities of higher things than are usually credited of Indians, — the inveterate and ferocious animosities of the Pawnees toward the Brulé Sioux have been so far sacrificed to the requirements of the government and the personal entreaties of their agent, that the past summer witnessed the phenomenon, astonishing to all who were cognizant of the deadly feuds existing for generations between these tribes, of Pawnees and Brulés hunting almost side by side, the camp-fires of both being distinctly visible upon the same plain, without a murder being committed, or so much as a horse stolen, by either party.

If, then, we may assume that Indian civilization is not altogether impossible, let us inquire what should be the policy of the government towards the Indian tribes when they cease to be dangerous to our frontier population, and to oppose the progress of settlement, either by violence or by menace. In such a discussion, we are bound to have a reasonable consideration for the interests of the white man as well as for the rights of the red man, but above all to defer to whatever experience declares in respect to the conditions most favorable to the growth of self-respect and self-restraint in minds so strangely and unfortunately constituted as is the mind of the North American Indian.

First. The reservation system should be made the general and permanent policy of the government. By this is meant something more than that the Indians should not be robbed of their lands in defiance of treaty stipulations, or that the Indian title should be respected, and the Indians maintained in possession until they can be made ready to cede their lands to the government, or to sell them, with the consent of the government, to the whites. The proposition is that the United States, as the only power competent to receive such lands by cession, or to authorize their sale, should formally establish the principle of separation and seclusion, without reference to the wishes either of the Indians or of encroaching whites; should designate by law an ample and suitable reservation for each tribe and band not entitled by treaty; and should, in any reductions thereafter requiring to be made, provide that such reductions shall be by cutting off distinct portions from the outside, and not in such a way as to allow veins of white settlement to be injected, no matter whether along a stream or along a railway.

The principle of secluding Indians from whites for the good of both races is established by an overwhelming preponderance of authority. There are no mysterious reasons why this policy should be adopted: the considerations which favor it are plain and incontestable. The first is the familiar one, that the Indian is unfortunately disposed to submit himself to the lower and baser elements of civilized society, and to acquire the vices and not the virtues of the whites. This need not be dwelt upon; but there is still another consideration even more important, yet not generally apprehended. It is that an Indian tribe is a singularly homogeneous body,* and, if not disturbed by the intrusion of alien and discordant elements, is susceptible of being governed and controlled with the greatest ease and effect. It is not necessary to point out the ways in which this peculiarity of the Indian character assists the agent of the government in his administration of a tribe, or to show how much more complete it makes his success, as, little by little, he is able, through the authority of the government, and the means of moral education at his disposal, to effect a change for the better in the public sentiment of the people under his charge.

The number of Indians now having reservations secured to them by law or treaty is approximately 180,000. The number of such reservations is 92, ranging in extent from 288 acres to 40,750 square miles, and aggregating 167,619 square miles. Of these reservations, 31, aggregating 2,693 square

* We are speaking of the tribe socially, not politically. Factions and faction wars are known to the Indian as well as to his betters.

miles, are east of the Mississippi River; 42, aggregating 144,838 square miles, are between the Mississippi and the Rocky Mountains; and 19, aggregating 20,068 square miles, are upon the Pacific slope. In addition to the above, 40,000 Indians, having no lands secured to them by treaty, have had reservations set apart for them by executive order, out of the public lands of the United States. The number of reservations thus set apart is 15, aggregating 59,544 square miles. The Indians thus located have, however, in the nature of the case, no assurance of their occupation of these lands beyond the pleasure of the executive.*

It must be evident to every one, on the simple statement of such facts as these, that the reservations, as at present constituted, do not consist with the permanent interests of either the Indian or the government. There are too many reservations: they occupy too much territory in the aggregate; and, what is worse, some of them unnecessarily obstruct the natural access of population to portions of territory not reserved, while others, by their neighborhood, render large tracts of otherwise available land undesirable for white

* Report on Indian Affairs, 1872, p. 84.

occupation. Indeed, it may be said that the present arrangement of reservations would constitute an almost intolerable affliction, were it to be maintained without change. Nor are the interests of the Indians any better served by the existing order. Many tribes, even were they disposed to agriculture, would not find suitable land within the limits assigned to them. Others are in a position to be incessantly disturbed and harassed by the whites. Others still, while they stand across the path of settlement, are themselves, by ill-considered treaty provisions, cut off from access to hunting-grounds, to fishing privileges, or to mountains abounding in natural roots and berries, which would be of the greatest value to them. When it is considered that the present body of reservations is the result of hundreds of treaties, made, too often, on the part of the government with ignorance and heedlessness, and on the part of the Indians with the childishness characteristic of the race, both parties being not infrequently deceived and betrayed by the interpreters employed; when it is considered, moreover, that many of these treaties have been negotiated in emergencies requiring immediate action, — it would be wonderful indeed if the scheme as it stood were not cumbersome and ineffective.

It is manifest, therefore, that the next five or ten years must witness a general recasting of the scheme of Indian reservations. This is not to be accomplished by confiscating the Indian title, but by exchange, by cession, and by consolidation. Let Congress provide the necessary authority, under the proper limitations, for the executive departments, and the adjustment desired can be reached easily and amicably.

Second. It is further evident, that, in recasting the scheme of reservations, the principal object should be, while preserving distinct the boundaries of every tribe, so to locate them that the territory assigned to the Indians west of the Mississippi shall constitute one or two grand reservations, with, perhaps, here and there a channel cut through, so to speak, by a railroad, so that the industries of the surrounding communities may not be unduly impeded. Such a consolidation of the Indian tribes into one or two great bodies would leave all the remaining territory of the United States open to settlement, without obstruction or molestation.

Shall there be one general reservation east of the Rocky Mountains, or two? This is likely to be the most important Indian question of the immediate future. On the one hand, the recommendations of the executive, contained in both the Messages of the President and the Annual Reports of the Secretary of the Interior, for the past two or three years, have strongly favored the plan of a single reservation for all the tribes, North and South, East and West, who are not in a condition to become at an early day citizens of the United States and take their land in severalty. The reservation upon which it is proposed to thus collect the Indians of the United States is at present known as the "Indian Territory," although it actually contains but about one-quarter of the Indian population of the country. This tract covers all the territory lying between the States of Arkansas and Missouri on the east, and the one-hundredth meridian on the west, and between the State of Kansas on the north, and the Red River, the boundary of the State of Texas, on the south; comprising about seventy thousand square miles, and embracing a large body of the best agricultural lands west of the Mississippi. Upon this tract, it is claimed, can be gathered and subsisted all the Indians within the administrative control of the government, except such as are manifestly becoming ripe for citizenship in the States and Territories where they are now found. Computing the maximum number likely, on the successful realization of this scheme to be thus concentrated, at two hundred and fifty thousand, and taking the available lands within the district, exclusive of barren plains, of flint hills and sand hills, at an aggregate of thirty million acres, we should have one hundred and twenty acres for each man, woman, and child to be provided for.

On the other hand, the original plan of Indian colonization, as contained in the report of Secretary Calhoun, accompanying the message of President Monroe, Jan. 27, 1825, contemplated two general reservations, — one in the North-west for the Indians of Algonquin and Iroquois stock, and another (being the present Indian Territory) in the South-west for the Appalachian Indians. The ethnographical symmetry of that plan has been hopelessly violated by the introduction into the Indian Territory, and even the incorporation with the Southern tribes, of individuals, broken bands, and even entire tribes, originally from the North and North-east. The bulk of the Shawnees, an Algonquin tribe, are actually incorporated with the Cherokees; two hundred of the Senecas, the very flower of the conquering Iroquois,* occupy a small reservation in the north-eastern part of the Territory; while the remnants of the Quapaws, Ottawas, Peorias, Kaskaskias, Weas,

* The popular and doubtless the correct use of the word "Iroquois" confines it to the Five Nations (subsequently the Six Nations) of New York, which during the third quarter of the seventeenth century destroyed or dispersed successively the Hurons or Wyandots, the nation called (for the want of a more characteristic name) the Neutral Nation, the Andastes of the Susquehanna, and the Eries. These four large and important peoples were closely kindred to the Five Nations; and the term "Iroquois" was long applied to this entire family of tribes. Later in the history of the continent, it embraced only the Five (or Six) Nations for the best of good reasons, as this formidable confederacy had practically annihilated all the other branches of the family. The career of the Iroquois was simply terrific. Between 1649 and 1672 they had, as stated, accomplished the ruin of the four tribes of their own blood, containing in the aggregate a population far more numerous than their own. A feeble remnant, a few score in number, of the Wyandots, now survive, and are represented at Washington by an exceptionally shabby white man, who has received the doubtful honor of adoption into the tribe. These are all the recognizable remains of a nation once estimated to contain thirty thousand. The names of the Eries, the Andastes, and the Neutral Nation do not appear in any treaty with the United States. Many, doubtless, from all these tribes fled to Canada. Considerable numbers were also, according to the custom of the Five Nations, adopted by the conquerors to make good the waste of war.

Nor did the Iroquois wait to complete the subjugation of their own kindred, before turning their arms against their Algonquin

Piankeshaws, Pottawatomies, and of the Sacs and Foxes,—all Algonquin tribes,—are found injected at various points along the northern and eastern frontier. At the same time, the south-

neighbors. The Delawares (Lenni Lenape, or Original Men) were subjugated almost coincidently with the Hurons; and the same year which brought the downfall of the Andastes witnessed the expulsion of the Shawnees from the valley of the Ohio. Re-enforced in 1712 by the Tuscaroras, a warlike tribe from the South, the Five Nations (now become the Six Nations) carried their conquests east and west, north and south. The tribes confronting the invaders in New England, New Jersey, Pennsylvania, and Virginia were continually disturbed and distracted by their incursions. Taking the part of the English in the wars against the French, they shook all Canada with the fear of their arms, while to the west they extended their sway to the Straits of Michilimackinac and the entrance to Lake Superior. The height of their fame was at the close of the Old French War in 1763. Their decline and downfall, as a power upon the continent, followed with the briefest interval. Reduced by incessant fighting to seventeen hundred warriors, they took the part of England against the Colonies in 1775. The glorious and the terrible incidents of the Indian campaigns of the Revolution are familiar as household words. The peace of 1783 found the Iroquois broken, humbled, homeless, helpless, before the power of the United States, whose pensioners they then became and have since remained. The bulk of these tribes still reside in New York, while fragments of them are found in the extreme West, having removed under the treaty of 1838.

Such, in brief, is the history of the Iroquois. They were the scourge of God upon the aborigines of the continent, and were themselves used up, stock, lash, and snapper, in the tremendous western portion of the Territory is given up to tribes which are neither Algonquin, Iroquois, nor Appalachian in their original, but are of the races living immemorially beyond the Mississippi. It will thus appear that nothing like an ethnographical distribution of tribes has been attempted; and, indeed, these distinctions have long ceased, with the Indians themselves, to be of the slightest significance. But many of the physiological and practical reasons urged by Secretary Calhoun for a double Indian reservation still remain in full force. Nor does this scheme rest upon his authority alone. The Peace Commission of 1867 and 1868, consisting of Indian Commissioner Taylor, Senator Henderson, Gens. Sherman, Harney, Terry, and Augur, of the army, and Messrs. Sanborn and Tappan, concurred in the

flagellation which was administered through them to almost every branch, in turn, of the great Algonquin family. It will not do to say, that, but for the Iroquois, the settlement of the country by the whites would not have taken place; yet assuredly that settlement would have been longer delayed, and have been finally accomplished with far greater expense of blood and treasure, had not the Six Nations, not knowing what they did, gone before in savage blindness and fury, destroying or driving out tribe after tribe which with them might, for more than one generation at least, have stayed the western course of European invasion.

recommendation of two reservations for tribes east of the Rocky Mountains.

We are disposed to hold, not only that the reason of the case inclines to the plan of two general reservations, but that the matter will be settled practically in that way by the aversion and horror which the Northern Indians feel at the thought of moving to the South. Regarding the Indian Territory, as they do, though with no sufficient reason, as the graveyard of their race, there is ground for apprehension that, if the project be too suddenly sprung upon them, or pressed too far, the repugnance of some of these tribes may culminate in outbreaks like those with which the Black Hawk and Seminole wars commenced. There can, however, be no objection to the experiment being tried in such a way as not to endanger the peace. Certain of the Northern tribes, notably the confederated Cheyennes and Arapahoes, and the confederated Arickarees and Mandans, manifest much less antipathy to removal than others, by reason of their relationship to Indians South, or of exceptional inconveniences sustained in their present location. If such tribes could be amicably induced to go to the Indian Territory, their experiences, if fortunate, might serve in time to remove the prejudices existing among the Northern Indians generally.

Third. The intrusion of whites upon lands reserved to Indians should be provided against by legislation suited to the necessities of the case. By the Indian Intercourse Act of 1834 it was made a criminal offence to enter without authority the limits of any Indian reservation; and the prohibition was enforced by penalties adequate to the situation at that time. This provision, however, was aimed at individual intruders, rather than at organized expeditions completely equipped for offence or defence, and strong enough to maintain themselves against considerable bands of the savages, or the ordinary *posse comitatus* of a distant Territory. It is in the latter form that the invasion of Indian country now generally takes place;* and for the purpose of resisting such

* The impudent character of these invasions will be best shown by a recital of the facts in two cases occurring within the year. In 1870–71 the Osages living in Kansas sold their lands under authority of the government, and accepted a reservation, in lieu thereof, in the Indian Territory. Scarcely had they turned their faces towards their new home when a sort of race began between them and some hundreds of whites, which may be described, in the language of boys, as having for its object "to see which should get there first." In October, 1871, the

organized lawlessness, the Act of 1834 is far from sufficient. The executive may, it is true, in an extreme case, and by the exercise of one of the

agent reported that five hundred whites were on the Osage lands, and actually in possession of the Osage village, while the rightful owners were encamped outside. Orders having been issued from the War Department for the removal of these intruders, political pressure was brought to bear upon the executive to prevent the orders from being carried into effect. This effort failing, delay was asked, in view of the hardships to be anticipated from a removal so near winter. This indulgence having been granted, the number of the trespassers continued to increase through the winter, in spite of the notice publicly given of the intentions of the government: so that in the spring of 1872 the military authorities found fifteen hundred persons on the Osage lands in defiance of law. On this occasion, however, the land-robbers had failed in their calculations. The government was in earnest; and the squatters were extruded by the troops of the Department of the Missouri.

The other instance referred to is that of an expedition projected and partially organized in Dakota, in 1872, for the purpose of penetrating the Black Hills, for mining and lumbering. Public meetings at which Federal officials attended were held, to create the necessary amount of public enthusiasm; and an invasion of Indian territory was imminent, which would, beyond peradventure, have resulted in a general Sioux war. In this case the emergency was such that the executive acted with great promptness. A proclamation was issued warning evil-disposed persons of the determination of the government to prevent the outrage; and troops were put in position to deal effectively with the marauders. This proved sufficient; and the Black Hills expedition was abandoned.

highest acts of authority, make proclamation forbidding such combinations, and enforce the same by movements of troops, as would be done in the case of a threatened invasion of the soil of a neighboring friendly state. But this remedy is of such a violent nature, the odium and inconvenience occasioned thereby are so great, and the lawful limits of official action in such a resort are so ill-defined, that the executive is most unlikely to make use of it, except in rare and extreme cases. The eagerness of the average American citizen of the Territories for getting upon Indian lands amounts to a passion. The ruggedest flint hill of the Cherokees or Sioux is sweeter to him than the greenest pasture which lies open to him under the homestead laws of the United States. There is scarcely one of the ninety-two reservations at present established on which white men have not effected a lodgement: many swarm with squatters, who hold their place by intimidating the rightful owners; while in more than one case the Indians have been wholly dispossessed, and are wanderers upon the face of the earth. So far have these forms of usurpation been carried at times in Kansas, that an Indian reservation there might be defined as that portion of the soil of the

State on which the Indians have no rights whatsoever.

Now, while it cannot be denied that there is something in all this suggestive of the reckless daring and restless enterprise to which the country owes so much of its present greatness, it is yet certain that such intrusion upon Indian lands is in violation of the faith of the United States, endangers the peace (as it has more than once enkindled war), and renders the civilization of tribes and bands thus encroached upon almost hopeless. The government is bound, therefore, in honor and in interest, to provide ample security for the integrity of Indian reservations; and this can only be done by additional and most stringent legislation.

Fourth. The converse of the proposition contained under the preceding head is equally true and equally important. Indians should not be permitted to abandon their tribal relations, and leave their reservations to mingle with the whites, except upon express authority of law. We mean by this something more than that a "pass system" should be created for every tribe under the control of the government, to prevent individual

Indians from straying away for an occasional debauch at the settlements. It is essential that the right of the authorities to keep members of any tribe upon the reservation assigned to them, and to arrest and return such as may from time to time wander away and seek to ally themselves with the whites, should be definitely established, and the proper forms and methods of procedure in such cases be fixed and prescribed by law. Without this, whenever these people become restive under compulsion to labor, they will break away in their old roving spirit, and stray off in small bands to neighboring communities. No policy of industrial education and restraint can be devised to meet the strong hereditary disinclination of the Indian to labor and to frugality which will not, in its first courses, tend to make him dissatisfied and rebellious. Nothing but the knowledge that he must stay on his reservation, and do all that is there prescribed for him; that he will not be permitted to throw off his connection with his people, and stray away to meet his own fate, unprovided, uninstructed, and unrestrained, — will, under any adequate system of moral and industrial correction and education, prevent a general breaking-up of Indian communities, and the formation of Indian gypsy-camps all over the frontier States and Territories, to be sores upon the public body, and an intolerable affliction to the future society of those communities.

Fifth. A rigid reformatory control should be exercised by the government over the lives and manners of the Indians of the several tribes, particularly in the direction of requiring them to learn and practise the arts of industry, at least until one generation shall have been fairly started on a course of self-improvement. Merely to disarm the savages, and to surround them by forces which it is impossible for them to resist, leaving it to their own choice how miserably they will live, and how much they shall be allowed to escape work, is to render it highly probable that the great majority of the now roving Indians will fall hopelessly into a condition of pauperism and petty crime.

"Unused to manual labor, and physically disqualified for it by the habits of the chase, unprovided with tools and implements, without forethought and without self-control, singularly susceptible to evil influences, with strong animal appetites, and no intellectual tastes or aspirations to hold those appetites in check, it would be to assume more than would be taken for granted of any white race under the same conditions, to expect that the wild Indians will become industrious and frugal except through a severe course of industrial instruction and exercise under restraint."—*Report on Indian Affairs*, 1872, p. 11.

The right of the government to exact, in this particular, all that the good of the Indian and the good of the general community may require is not to be questioned. The same supreme law of the public safety which to-day governs the condition of eighty thousand paupers and forty thousand criminals, within the States of the Union, affords ample authority and justification for the most extreme and decided measures which may be adjudged necessary to save this race from itself, and the country from the intolerable burden of pauperism and crime which the race, if left to itself, will certainly inflict upon a score of future States.

Sixth. The provision made by the government for the partial subsistence of Indian tribes through the long and painful transition from the hunter life to the agricultural state, for their instruction and equipment in industrial pursuits, and for starting them finally on a course of full self-support and economical independence, should be liberal and generous, even to an extreme. The experiment should not be allowed to encounter any chances of failure which may be avoided by expenditure of money. The claim of the Indian in this respect is of the strongest. He has no right to prevent the settling of this continent by a race which has not only the power to conquer, but the disposition to improve and adorn the land which he has suffered to remain a wilderness. Yet to some royalty upon the product of the soil the Indian is incontestably entitled as the original occupant and possessor. The necessities of civilization may justify a somewhat summary treatment of his rights, but cannot justify a confiscation of them. The people of the United States can never without dishonor refuse to respect two considerations, — first, that the Indians were the original occupants and owners of substantially all the territory embraced within our limits; that their title of occupancy has been recognized by all civilized powers having intercourse with them, and has been approved in nearly four hundred treaties concluded by the United States with individual tribes and bands; and, therefore, every tribe and band that is deprived of its roaming privilege and confined to a "diminished reservation" is clearly entitled to compensation, either directly or in the form of expenditures for its benefit: second, that, inasmuch as the progress of our industrial enterprise is fast cutting this people off from modes of livelihood entirely sufficient for them, and suited to them, and is leaving them without resource, they have a claim, on this account again, to temporary support and to such assistance as may be necessary to place them in a position to obtain a livelihood by means which shall be compatible with civilization.

"Had the settlements of the United States not been extended beyond the frontier of 1867, all the Indians of the continent would to the end of time have found upon the plains an inexhaustible supply of food and clothing. Were the westward course of population to be stayed at the barriers of to-day, notwithstanding the tremendous inroads made upon their hunting-grounds since 1867, the Indians would still have hope of life. But another such five years will see the Indians of Dakota and Montana as poor as the Indians of Nevada and Southern California; that is, reduced to an habitual condition of suffering from want of food. The freedom of expansion which is working these results is to us of incalculable value: to the Indian it is of incalculable cost." — *Report on Indian Affairs*, 1872, p. 10.

Seventh. It is, further, highly desirable, in order to avoid the possibility of an occasional failure in such provision for the immediate wants of the Indians, and for their advancement in the arts of life and industry, and also to secure comprehensiveness and consistency in the general scheme, that the endowments for the several tribes and bands should be capitalized and placed in trust for their benefit, out of the reach of accident or caprice. Annual appropriations for such purposes, according to the humor of Congress, will of necessity be far less effective for good than would an annual income of a much smaller amount, arising from permanent investments.

To a considerable extent this has already been effected. For not a few tribes and bands provision has been made by law and treaty which places them beyond the reach of serious suffering in the future, and which, if their income be judiciously administered, will afford them substantial assistance towards final self-support. Stocks to the value of $4,810,716.83⅔ are held by the Secretary of the Interior in trust for certain tribes; while credits to the aggregate amount of $5,905,474.59 are inscribed on the books of the United States Treasury in favor of the same or other tribes, on account of the sales of lands, or other consideration received by the government,* making a permanent endowment of nearly ten millions of dollars, the Indians sharing in the benefits thereof numbering in the aggregate nearly eighty thousand. Computing the average annual return from these funds at five and one-half per cent, we should have an assured income of five hundred and fifty thousand dollars a year, or about seven dollars for each man, woman, and child. Moreover, most of these tribes have still large bodies of lands which they can dispose of sooner or later, from which funds of twice the amount already secured may by honest and judicious management be realized; so that, taking these eighty thousand Indians as a body, they may be regarded as having a reasonable assurance of funds yielding an annual income of twenty dollars a head. Their general character and condition being considered, this may be accepted as an amply sufficient endowment, placing their future in their own hands, giving them all the opportunities and appliances that could reasonably be asked for them, and securing them against the calamities and reverses which inevitably beset the first stages of industrial progress.

* Report on Indian Affairs, 1872, p. 440.

Unfortunately, the same wise provision for the future has not been made in the case of other Indians who have ceded or surrendered to the government the main body of their lands. There is a painfully long list of tribes that have to show for their inheritance only a guaranty on the part of the United States of certain expenditures, more or less beneficial, for a series of years longer or shorter, as the case may be. The Report on Indian Affairs for 1872 (pp. 418–430) states the aggregate of future appropriations that will be required during a limited number of years to pay limited annuities at $15,819,310.46. The annuities covered by this computation have from one to twenty-seven years to run (the average term being about seven years), and embrace almost every variety of goods and services which human ingenuity could suggest. Many of the things stipulated to be given to the Indians, or to be done for them, are admirable in themselves, but far in advance of the present requirements of the tribes; and the expenditures involved are therefore perfectly useless. Other things would be well enough if the Indians could have every thing they wanted, but are absurd and mischievous as taking the place of what is absolutely essential to their well-being.

Of other things embraced in the schedule of annual appropriations, it can only be said that the Indians need them no more than a toad needs a pocket-book. For such waste of Indian moneys the responsibility rests in many cases upon the commissioners, who, on the part of the United States, negotiated the treaties under which these appropriations are annually made. Had they been half as solicitous for the future of the Indians as they were for the attainment of the immediate object of negotiation, the government would have been left free to apply the amounts, to be paid in consideration for cessions, in such manner as to make them of substantial benefit; or, better still, the amounts would have been capitalized, and a permanent income secured. As it is, many tribes now see approaching the termination of annuities which have for many years been paid them with the very minimum of advantage, and have no prospect beyond but that of being thrown, uninstructed and unprovided, upon their own barbarous resources.

Let us illustrate. A tribe makes a treaty with the United States, ceding the great body of their lands, and accepting a diminished reservation sufficient for their actual occupation. In consideration, it is provided that there shall be maintained upon the reservation, for the term of fifteen years, at the expense of the United States, a superintendent of teaching and two teachers, a superintendent of farming and two farmers, two millers, two blacksmiths, a tinsmith, a gunsmith, a carpenter, and a wagon and plough maker, with shops and material for all these mechanical services. This "little bill" is presumably made up without much reference to the peculiarities in character and condition of the tribe to be benefited by the expenditures involved. As soon as the treaty goes into effect, the United States in good faith fulfil their part of the bargain. The shops are built, the employees enlisted; and the government, through its agent, stands ready to civilize the Indians to almost any extent. But, unfortunately, the Indians are not ready to be civilized. The glow of industrial enthusiasm, which was created by the metaphorical eloquence of the commissioners in council dies away under the first experiment of hard work: an hour at the plough nearly breaks the back of the wild man wholly unused to labor: his pony, a little wilder still, jumps now on one side of the furrow and now on the other, and finally settles the question by kicking itself free of the galling harness, and disappears for the day. The Indian, a sadder and wiser man, betakes himself to the chase, and thereafter only visits the shops, maintained at so much expense by the government, to have his gun repaired, or to get a strap or buckle for his riding-gear. But still the treaty expenditures go on: the United States are every year loyally furnishing what has been stipulated; and the Indian is every year one instalment nearer the termination of all his claims upon the government. Meanwhile, population is closing around the reservation: the animals of the chase are disappearing before the presence of the white man, and the sound of the pioneer's axe: scantier and scantier grow the natural means of subsistence, fainter and fainter the attractions of the chase; and when at last hunger drives the Indian in to the agency, made ready by suffering to learn the white man's ways of life, the provisions of the treaty are well-nigh expired. One, three, or five years pass. All the instalments have been honorably paid: the appropriation committees of Congress, with sighs of relief, cross off the name of the tribe from the list of beneficiaries; and another body of Indians, uninstructed and unprovided, are left to shift for themselves.

The importance of the subject will justify us in dwelling so long upon it. Of the expenditures made within the last twenty years under treaty stipulations, probably not one-half has been directed to uses which the government would have chosen, had it been free to choose. It is most melancholy thus to see the scanty patrimony of this people squandered on worthless objects, or dissipated in efforts necessarily fruitless. The action of Congress at its last session, in authorizing the diversion of sums appropriated under treaty stipulations to other specific uses, at the discretion of the President and with the consent of the Indians, is a step in the right direction. But the time has come for a complete and comprehensive fiscal scheme, looking to the realization from Indian lands of the largest possible avails, and their capitalization and investment upon terms and conditions which will secure the future of the several tribes, so far as human wisdom may be able to fect this.

In addition to the lands held by the eighty thousand Indians who have already been spoken of as amply endowed, there are one hundred thousand square miles of territory yet secured by treaty to Indian tribes aggregating one hundred thousand persons. Besides these, forty thousand Indians enjoy, by executive order, the occupation of other sixty thousand square miles of territory, which, or the substantial equivalent of which, should be secured to them by law for their ultimate endowment. It is to these lands that such a fiscal scheme as has been indicated should be applied. The reservations assigned to tribes and bands are generally proportioned to the needs of the Indians in a roving state, with hunting and fishing as their chief means of subsistence. As the Indians change to agriculture, the effect is to contract the limits of actual occupation, rendering portions available for cession or sale, which with proper management may be so disposed of, without impairing the integrity of the reservation system, as to realize for nearly every tribe and band a fund equal, *per capita*, to that of many of the civilized tribes of the Indian Territory. But this cannot be done by helter-skelter or hap-hazard administration. The subject must be taken up as a whole, broadly considered, and intelligently treated, and the scheme which shall be adopted thereafter be regarded as not less sacred than the compromises of the Constitution, or than existing treaty obligations.

For the tribes and bands having no reservations secured to them, separate provision should be made. These number about fifty thousand persons, deduction being made of such as already have their lands in severalty, or as are hopelessly scattered among the settlements. Many of these tribes and bands might, with the assistance of the government, advantageously "buy themselves in" to the privileges of tribes already provided for, without involving any further donation of lands.

Where it is found impracticable thus to place the unprovided bands, the government should secure their location and endowment separately. Their right is no less clear than the right of other tribes which had the fortune to deal with the United States before Congress put an end to the treaty system. We have received the soil from them; and we have extinguished their only means of subsistence. Either consideration would be sufficient to require us, in simple justice, to find them a place and ways to live.

The foregoing constitute what we regard as the essential features of an Indian policy which shall seek positively and actively the reformation of life and manners among the Indians under the control of the government, as opposed to the policy of hastening the time when all these tribes shall be resolved into the body of our citizenship, without seclusion and without restraint, letting such as will, go to the dogs, letting such as can, find a place for themselves in the social and industrial order, the responsibility of the government or our people for the choice of either or the fate of either being boldly denied; suffering, meanwhile, without precaution and without fear, such debasement in blood and manners to be wrought upon the general population of the country as shall be incident to the absorption of this race, relying upon the inherent vigor of our stock to assimilate much and rid itself of more, until, in the course of a few human generations, the native Indians, as a pure race or a distinct people, shall have disappeared from the continent.

The reasons for maintaining that nothing less than a system of moral and industrial education and correction can discharge the government of its obligations to the Indians, or save the white population from an intolerable burden of pauperism, profligacy, and petty crime, have been presented sufficiently at length in this paper. The details of management and instruction need not be here discussed: most of them are within the administrative discretion of the department charged with Indian affairs; and, where power is wanting to the department, the good feeling of Congress may be safely trusted to give the necessary authority. But the points which have been presented are of vital consequence, and must, if the evils we apprehend are to be prevented, at an early date be embodied in legislation which shall provide means and penalties ample for its own enforcement.

Are the Indians destined to die out? Are we to make such provision as has been indicated, or such other as the wisdom or unwisdom of the country shall determine, for a vanishing race? Or are the original inhabitants of the continent to be represented in the variously and curiously composed population which a century hence will constitute the political body of the United States? If this is to be in any appreciable degree one of the elements of our future population, will it be by mixture and incorporation? Or will the Indian remain a distinct type in our museum of humanity, submitting himself to the necessities of a new condition, adapting himself, as he may be able to do, to the laws and customs of his conquerors, but preserving his own identity, and making his separate contribution to the life and manners of the nation?

The answers to these questions will depend very much on the course to be followed in the immediate future with respect to the tribes not yet embraced within the limits of States of the Union. If, for the want of a definite and positive policy of instruction and restraint, they are left to scatter under the pressure of hunger, the intrusion of squatters and prospectors, or the seductions of the settlements, there is little doubt that the number of Indians of full blood will rapidly diminish, and the race, as a pure race, soon become extinct. But nothing could be more disastrous than this method of ridding the country of an undesirable element. Not only would it be more cruel to the natives than a war of extermination; but it would entail in the course of its accomplishment a burden of vice, disease, pauperism, and crime upon a score of new States, more intolerable than perpetual alarms or unintermitted war.

But if, on the other hand, the policy of seclusion shall be definitely established by law and rigidly maintained, the Indians will meet their fate, whatever it may be, substantially as a whole and as a pure race. White men will still be found, so low in natural instincts, or so alienated by misfortunes and wrongs, as to be willing to abandon civilization, and hide themselves in a condition of life where no artificial wants are known, and in communities where public sentiment makes no demand upon any member for aught in the way of achievement or self-advancement. Here such men, even now to be found among the more remote and hostile tribes, will, unless the savage customs of adoption are severely discountenanced by law, find their revenge upon humanity, or escape the tyranny of social observance and requirement. Half-breeds, bearing the names of French, English, and American employees of fur and trading companies, or of refugees from criminal justice "in the settlements," are to be found in almost every tribe and band, however distant. Many of them, grown to man's estate, are among the most daring, adventurous, and influential members of the warlike tribes, seldom wholly free from suspicion on account of their relation on one side to the whites, yet, by the versatility of their talents and the recklessness of their courage, commanding the respect and the fear of the pure-bloods, and, however incapable of leading the savages in better courses, powerful in a high degree for mischief.

The white men, who, under the reservation system, are likely to become affiliated with Indian tribes as "squaw men," are, however, probably fewer than the Indian women who will be enticed away from their tribes to become the cooks and concubines of ranchmen. One is surprised even now, while travelling in the Territories, to note the number of cabins around which, in no small families, half-breed children are playing. However moralists or sentimentalists may look upon connections thus formed by men who are in effect beyond the pale of society and of law, they constitute already a distinct feature of border life; nor is any statute likely to prevent Indian women occasionally thus straying from their own people, or to compel their return so long as they are under the protection of white men.

But, while the seclusion of the two races upon the frontier is certain to be thus broken in instances which will form no inconsiderable exception to the rule, the substantial purity of blood may be maintained by an early adjustment of reservations, the concentration of tribes, and the exercise of disciplinary control by their agents over the movements of wandering parties. Whether, in such an event, the Indians, thus left to meet their fate by themselves, with reasonable provision by the government for their instruction in the arts of life and industry, will waste away in strength and numbers, is a question quite too large to be entered upon here. Popular beliefs and scientific opinion undoubtedly contemplate the gradual if not the speedy decline of Indian tribes when deprived of their traditional freedom of movement, pent up within limits comparatively narrow, and compelled to uncongenial occupations. But there is grave reason to doubt whether these causes are certain to operate in any such degree as to involve the practical extinction of the race within that immediate future on which we are accustomed to speculate, and for which we feel bound to make provision. On the contrary, there are many considerations and not a few facts which fairly intimate a possibility that the Indian may bear restriction as well as the negro has borne emancipation; and, like the negro, after a certain inevitable loss consequent upon a change so great and violent, adapt himself with increased vitality to new conditions. It is true that the transition, compulsory as to a great degree it must be, from

9

a wholly barbarous condition of life, which remains to be effected for the eighty to one hundred thousand Indians still outside the practical scope of the Indian service, is likely to further reduce, for some years to come, the aggregate number of this race; but it is not improbable that this will be coincident with a steady increase among the tribes known as civilized.

In the foregoing discussion of the policy to be pursued in dealing with the Indians of the United States, there has been no disposition to mince matters, or to pick expressions. The facts and considerations deemed essential have been presented bluntly. Some who cannot bear to hear Indians spoken of as savages, or to contemplate the chastisement of marauding bands, may blame our frankness. But we hold fine sentiments to be out of place in respect to a matter like this, which in the present is one of life and death to thousands of our own flesh and blood, and in the future one of incalculable importance to a score of States yet to be formed out of the territory over which the wild tribes of to-day are roaming in fancied independence. The country has a right to the whole naked truth, — to learn what security our fellow-citizens have for their lives, and also to learn what becomes of the seven millions of dollars annually collected in taxes and disbursed on Indian account.

If the case has been fairly presented, it will doubtless appear to our readers, that, so far as the hostile and semi-hostile Indians are concerned, the government is merely temporizing with a gigantic evil, pocketing its dignity from considerations of humanity and economy, and awaiting the operation of causes both sure and swift, which must within a few years reduce the evil to dimensions in which it can be dealt with on principles more agreeable to the ideas and ways of our people.

For the rest, it will be seen that the United States have, without much order or comprehension, but with a vast amount of good-will, undertaken enterprises involving considerable annual expenditures for the advancement of individual tribes and bands, but that the true permanent scheme for the management and instruction of the whole body of Indians within the control of the government is yet to be created. Let it not for a moment be pretended that the prospect is an agreeable one. Congress and the country might well wish to be well rid of the matter. No

subject of legislation could be more perplexing and irritating; nor can the outlay involved fail for many years to be a serious burden upon our industry. But the nation cannot escape its responsibility for the future of this race, soon to be thrown in entire helplessness upon our protection. Honor and interest urge the same imperative claim. An unfaithful treatment will only make the evil worse, the burden heavier. In good faith and good feeling we must take up this work of Indian civilization, and, at whatever cost, do our whole duty by this most unhappy people. Better that we should entail a debt upon our posterity on Indian account, were that necessary, than that we should leave them an inheritance of shame. We may have no fear that the dying curse of the red man, outcast and homeless by our fault, will bring barrenness upon the soil that once was his, or dry the streams of the beautiful land that, through so much of evil and of good, has become our patrimony; but surely we shall be clearer in our lives, and freer to meet the glances of our sons and grandsons, if in our generation we do justice and show mercy to a race which has been impoverished that we might be made rich.

INDIAN CITIZENSHIP.*

THE proper treatment of the Indian question requires that we deal with the issues arising out of the peculiar relations of the aboriginal tribes of the continent to the now dominant race, in much the same spirit — profoundly philanthropic at bottom, but practical, sceptical, and severe in the discussion of methods and in the maintenance of administrative discipline — with which all Christian nations, and especially the English-speaking nations, have learned to meet the kindred difficulties of pauperism. It is in no small degree the lack of such a spirit in the conduct of Indian affairs, which has rendered the efforts and expenditures of our government for the advancement of the race so ineffectual in the past; and for this the blame attaches mainly to the want of correct information and of settled convictions respecting

* From The International Review, May, 1874.

this subject, among our people at large. So long as the country fluctuates in an alternation of sentimental and brutal impulses, according as the wrongs done to the Indian or the wrongs done by him are at the moment more distinctly in mind, it cannot be wondered at that Congress should be reluctant to undertake the re-organization of the Indian service on any large and lasting plan, or that the Indian Office should hesitate to cut out for itself more work than it can look to make up in the interval between sessions.

What, to take a recent and memorable instance, would have been the fate of any scheme of Indian legislation which was at its parliamentary crisis when the murder of Gen. Canby occurred? The work of years might well have been undone under the popular excitement attendant upon that atrocious deed. Yet it would be quite as rational to denounce the established systems for the care and control of the insane, and to turn all the inmates of our asylums loose upon the community because one maniac had in an access of frenzy murdered his keeper, as it would have been to abandon the established Indian policy of the government, the only fault of which is that it is incomplete, on account of any thing that Capt. Jack and his companions might do in their furious despair. The more atrocious their deed, the more conspicuous the justification of the system of care and control from which this one small band of desperadoes had for the moment broken free to work such horrid mischief. Yet there is much reason to believe, that, had the Indian service at that time depended, as every service must once a year come to depend, on the votes of Congressmen, it would have failed, temporarily at least, for the want of them. Nor is it only acts of exceptional ferocity on the part of marauding bands, which have sufficed to check all the gracious impulses of the national compassion. The reasons which have existed in the public mind in favor of the Indian policy of the government have not always been found of a sufficiently robust and practical nature to withstand the weariness of sustained effort, and the inevitable disappointments of sanguine expectation; and thus the service has at times suffered from the general indifference scarcely less than from the sharpest revulsions of public feeling.

Much has been said within the past three years, of the Indian policy of the administration; and, if by this is meant that the policy of the government in dealing with the Indians has become more and more one of administration, and less and less one of law, the phrase, with the exception of an article too many, is well enough. As matter of fact, the sole Indian policy of the United States deserving the name was adopted early in the century; and it is only of late years that it has been seriously undermined by the current of events; while it is within the duration of the present administration that the blow has been struck by legislation, at the already tottering structure, which has brought it nearly to its fall.

To throw upon a dozen religious and benevolent societies the responsibility of advising the executive in the appointment of the agents of the Indian service is not a policy. To buy off a few bands, more insolent than the rest, by a wholesale issue of subsistence and the lavish bestowal of presents, without reference to the disposition of the savages to labor for their own support, and even without reference to the good or ill desert of individuals, — this, though doubtless expedient in the critical situation of our frontier population, is the merest expediency, not in any sense a policy. Yet the two features specified have been the only ones that have been added to the scheme of Indian control during the continuance of the present administration; while, on the other side, an irreparable breach has been effected in that scheme by the action of powerful social forces, as well as by the direct legislative contravention of its most vital principle.

From the earliest settlement of the country by the whites, down to 1817, the Colonies, and afterwards the thirteen States, met the emergencies of Indian contact as they arose. The parties to negotiation were often ill-defined, and the forms of procedure much as happened. Not only did each Colony, prior to 1774, conduct its own Indian relations, generally with little or no reference to the engagements or the interests of its white neighbors; but isolated settlements and even enterprising individuals made their own peace with the savages, or received the soil by deed from its native proprietors. Nor on the part of the Indians was there much more regard for strict legitimacy. Local chieftains were not infrequently ready to convey away lands that did not belong to them; and when a Colony grown powerful wished a pretext for usurpation, almost any Indian would do to make a treaty with or get a title from. It is scarcely necessary to say of negotiations thus conducted, that they embraced no general scheme of Indian relations; that they aimed invariably at the accomplishment of immediate and more or less local objects, and often attained these at the cost of much embarrassment in the future, and even at the expense of neighboring settlements and colonies.

Throughout the history of Colonial transactions, we find few traces of any thing like impatience of the claims of the Indians to equality in negotiation and in intercourse. Neither the power nor the character of the aborigines was then despised as now. Strong in his native illusions, his warlike prestige unbroken, the Indian still retained all that natural dignity of bearing which has been found so impressive even in his decline. The early literature of the country testifies to the disposition of the people to hold the more romantic view of the Indian character, even where the animosities of race were deadliest; nor does it seem that the general sentiment of the Colonies regarded the necessity of treating on equal terms with the great confederacies of that day as in any degree more derogatory than the civilized powers of Europe in the same period esteemed the necessity of maintaining diplomatic relations with the great Cossack power of the North. Indeed, the treaty with the Delawares in 1778 actually contemplated the formation of a league of friendly tribes under the hegemony of the Delawares, to constitute the fourteenth State of the confederation then in arms against Great Britain, with a proportional representation in Congress. And this was proposed, not by men accustomed to see negroes voting at the polls, and even sitting in the Senate of the United States, but by our conservative and somewhat aristocratic ancestors.

But after the establishment of our national independence, incidental to which had been the destruction of the warlike power of the "Six Nations," the nearest and most formidable of all the confederacies known to Colonial history, we note a louder tone taken — as was natural enough — with the aboriginal tribes, a greater readiness to act aggressively, and an increasing confidence in the competency of the white race to populate the whole of this continent. Earlier Indian wars had been in a high sense a struggle for life on the part of the infant settlements: they had been engaged in reluctantly, after being postponed by every expedient and every artifice; but the conquest of the territory north-west of the Ohio appears to have been entered upon more from a statesmanlike comprehension of the wants of the united and expanding republic, than from the pressure of immediate danger. It was but natural that the concentration of the fighting power of the States, the consciousness of a common destiny, and the cession of the western territory to the general government, should create an impatience of Indian occupation which neither the separate Colonies nor the States, struggling for independence, had felt. Yet even so we do not find that, from 1783 to 1817, the United States did much more than meet the exigency most nearly and clearly at hand.

In the latter year, however, the negotiations for a removal of the Cherokees west of the Mississippi, although commenced under strong pressure from the much-afflicted State of Georgia, and at the time without contemplation of an extension of the system to tribes less immediately in the path of settlement, mark the beginnings of a distinct Indian policy. In 1825 the scheme for the general deportation of the Indians east of the Mississippi was fairly inaugurated in the presidency of Mr. Monroe; Mr. Calhoun, his secretary of war, proposing the details of the measure. In 1834 the policy thus inaugurated was completed by the passage of the Indian Intercourse Act, though large numbers still remained to be transported West.

The features of this policy were first, the removal of the tribes beyond the limits of settlement; second, the assignment to them in perpetuity, under solemn treaty sanctions, of land sufficient to enable them to subsist by fishing and hunting, by stock-raising, or by agriculture, according to their habits and proclivities; third, their seclusion from the whites by stringent laws forbidding intercourse; fourth, the government of the Indians through their own tribal organizations, and according to their own customs and laws.

This policy, the character and relations of the two races being taken into account, we must pronounce one of sound and far-reaching statesmanship, notwithstanding that an advance of population altogether unprecedented in history has already made much of it obsolete, and rendered necessary a general re-adjustment of its details.

The first event which impaired the integrity of the scheme of President Monroe was the flight of the Mormons, under the pressure of social persecution, across the Plains in 1847. The success of this people in treating with the Indians has often been noted, and has been made the occasion of many unjust reflections upon the United States, as if a popular government, giving, both of necessity and of choice, the largest liberty to pioneer enterprise, could be reasonably expected to preserve peaceful relations with remote bands of savages as effectively as a political and religious despotism, keeping its membership compact and close in hand. But, while the Mormons have certainly been successful in maintaining good terms with the natives of the plains, it is not so certain that their influence upon the Indians has been advantageous to the government, or to the white settlers not of the church. It clearly has been for their interest to attach the natives to themselves rather than to the government; it clearly has been in their power to direct a great many agencies to that end; and it will probably require more faith in Mormon virtue than the majority of us possess to keep alive much of a doubt that they have actually done so. We certainly have the opinion of many persons well informed that it has been the constant policy of the Latter-Day Saints to teach the Indians to look to them rather than to the government as their benefactors and their protectors; to represent, as far as possible through agents and interpreters in their interest, the goods and supplies received from the United States as derived from the bounty of the church; to stir up, for special purposes or for general ends, troubles between the natives and the encroaching whites, east, west, and south; and, finally, so to alienate from the government and attach to themselves the Utes, Shoshones and Bannocks, as to assure themselves of their aid in the not improbable event of a last desperate struggle for life with the power of the United States.

The next event historically which tended to the disruption of the policy of seclusion was the discovery of gold upon the Pacific slope, which in three years replaced the few insinuating priests and indolent *rancheros*, who had previously formed the white population of the coast, with a hundred thousand eager gold-hunters. That the access of such a population — bold, adventurous, prompt to violence, reckless, and too often wantonly unjust and cruel — should stir up trouble and strife with the sixty thousand natives, upon whom they pressed at every point in their eager search for the precious metals, was a thing of course. The Oregon War followed, and occasional affairs like that at Ben Wright's Cave, leaving a heritage of hate from which such fruits as the recent Modoc War are not inaptly gathered.

In 1855–6 occurred the great movement, mainly under a political impulse, which carried population beyond the Missouri. In two or three years the tribes and bands which were native to Kansas and Nebraska, as well as those which had been removed from States east of the Mississippi, were suffering the worst effects of white intrusion. Of the Free-State party, not a few zealous members seemed disposed to compensate themselves for their benevolent efforts on behalf of the negro by crowding the Indian to the wall; while the slavery propagandists steadily maintained their consistency by impartially persecuting the members of both the inferior races.

Thus far we have shown how, instead of the natural boundary between the races which was contemplated in the establishment of the Indian policy of the government under Pres. Monroe, two lines of settlement had, prior to 1860, been pushed against the Indians, — one eastward from the Pacific, one westward from the Missouri, driving the natives in many cases from the soil guaranteed to them by treaty, and otherwise leaving them at a hundred points in dangerous contact with a border population not apt to be nice in its sense of justice, or slow to retaliate real or fancied injuries; while, during the same period, a colony of religious fanatics, foreign to the faith, and very largely also to the blood, of our people, was planted in the very heart of the Indian country, with passions strongly aroused against the government, and with interests opposed to the peace and security of the frontier.

But it was not until after the Civil War that the progress of events dealt its heaviest blow at the policy of Indian seclusion. In 1867–8 the great plough of industrial civilization drew its deep furrow across the continent, from the Missouri to the Pacific, as a sign of dissolution to the immemorial possessors of the soil. Already the Pacific Railroad has brought changes which, without it, might have been delayed for half a century. Not only has the line of settlement been made continuous from Omaha to Sacramento, so far as the character of the soil will permit; but from a score of points upon the railroad population has gone north and gone south, following up the courses of the streams, and searching out every trace of gold upon the mountains, till recesses have been penetrated which five years ago were scarcely known to trappers and guides, and lodgement has been effected upon many even of the more remote reservations. The natural effects of this introduction by the railroad of white population into the Indian country have not yet been wholly wrought. There are still reservations where the seclusion of the Indians is practically maintained by the ill-repressed hostility of tribes; some, where the same result is secured by the barrenness or inaccessibility of the regions in which they are situated: but it is evident that the lapse of another such five years will find every reservation between the Mississippi River and the Rocky Mountains surrounded, and to a degree penetrated, by prospectors and pioneers, miners, ranchmen, or traders. Against the intrusion of these classes, in the numbers in which they are now appearing in the Indian country, the Intercourse Act of 1834 is wholly ineffective. It was an admirable weapon against the single intruder: it avails nothing against the lawless combinations of squatter territories.

While the movements of population have thus in great part destroyed, and threaten soon utterly to destroy, at once the seclusion in which it was hoped the native tribes might find opportunity for the development of their better qualities, and the natural resources to which, in the long interval that must precede the achievement of true industrial independence by a people taught through centuries of barbarous traditions to despise labor, the Indian might look for subsistence, Congress in 1871 struck the severest blow that remained to be given to the Indian policy, in its fourth great feature, — that of the self-government of tribes according to their own laws and customs, — by declaring that "Hereafter no Indian nation or tribe within the territory of the United States shall be acknowledged or recognized as an independent nation, tribe, or power, with whom the United States may contract by treaty."

In the face of three hundred and eighty-two treaties with Indian tribes, ratified by the Senate as are treaties with foreign powers, this may perhaps be accepted as quite the most conspicuous illustration in history of the adage, "Circumstances alter cases." * Since Anthony Wayne received

* The doctrine of a *vanishing* Indian nationality was strongly insisted on by Mr. Justice McLean in his opinion in Worcester *vs.* the State of Georgia: —

"If a tribe of Indians shall become so degraded or reduced in numbers as to lose the power of self-government, the protection of the local law, of necessity, must be extended over them. The point at which this exercise of power by a State would be the cession of pretty much the whole State of Ohio from the Wyandots, Delawares, and Shawnees, times have indeed changed; and it is fitting that we should change with them. The declaration of Congress is well enough on grounds of justice and national honor; but it none the less aims a deadly blow at the tribal autonomy which was made a vital part of the original scheme of Indian control. The declaration cited does not in terms deny the self-sufficiency of the tribe for the purposes of internal self-government; but the immediate necessary effect of it is further to weaken the already waning power of the chiefs, while Congress yet fails to furnish any substitute for their authority, — either by providing for the

proper need not now be considered, if, indeed, it be a judicial question. . . . But, if a contingency shall occur which shall render the Indians who reside in a State incapable of self-government, either by moral degradation or a reduction of their numbers, it would undoubtedly be in the power of a State government to extend over them the ægis of its laws." —6 *Peters*, pp. 593–4.

If, as would appear, Mr. Justice McLean by this intends that a State may exercise such discretion so long as the United States continue to recognize the tribal organization, however feeble or corrupt it may in fact be, the doctrine is flatly contradicted by that of the Supreme Court in the Kansas Indians. —5 *Wallace*, 737.

organization of the tribes on more democratic principles, with direct responsibility to the government, or by arming the Indian agents with magisterial powers adequate to the exigency.

Under the traditional policy of the United States, the Indian agent was a minister resident to a "domestic dependent nation." The Act of March 3, 1871, destroys the nationality, and leaves the agent in the anomalous position of finding no authority within the tribe to which he can address himself, yet having in himself no legal authority over the tribe or the members of it. It is true, that, as matter of fact, agents, some in greater and some in less degree, continue to exercise control after a fashion over the movements of tribes and bands. This is partly due to the force of habit, partly to superior intelligence, partly to the discretion which the agent exercises in the distribution of the government's bounty; but every year the control becomes less effectual, and agents and chiefs complain more and more that they cannot hold the young braves in check.

The above recital, however tedious, has been necessary in order to set fairly forth the actual condition of the scheme of seclusion, which is still, in profession and seeming, the policy of the government. It must be evident from the recital, that the purposes of this policy are not being answered, and that the increasing difficulties of the situation in the wider and closer contact of the two races will soon compel Congress to review the whole field of Indian affairs, and establish relations, which, if they cannot in the nature of things be permanent, will at least have reference to the facts of the present, and the probabilities of the immediate future. Whenever Congress shall take up in earnest this question of the disposition to be made of the Indian tribes, its choice will clearly be between two antagonistic schemes, — seclusion and citizenship. Either the government must place the Indians upon narrower reservations, proportioned to their requirements for subsistence by agriculture, and no longer by the chase, — reservations which shall be located with the view of avoiding as much as possible the contact of the races, and working as little hindrance as may be to the otherwise free development of population; and around these put up the barriers of forty years ago, re-enforced as the changed circumstances seem to require: or the government must prepare to receive the Indians into the body of the people, freely accepting, for them and for the general community, all the dangers and inconveniences of personal contact and legal equality. No middle ground is tenable. If substantial seclusion is not to be maintained, at any cost, by the sequestration of tribes and by the rigid prohibition of intercourse, it is worse than useless to keep up the forms of reservations and non-intercourse. Many tribes are already as fully subject to all the debasing influences of contact with the whites as they could be if dispersed among the body of citizens; while yet they are without any of the advantages popularly attributed to citizenship.

It requires no deep knowledge of human nature, and no very extensive review of Congressional legislation, to assure us that many and powerful interests will oppose themselves to a re-adjustment of the Indian tribes between the Missouri and the Pacific, under the policy of seclusion and non-intercourse. Railroad enterprises, mining enterprises, and land enterprises of every name, will find any scheme that shall be seriously proposed to be quite the most objectionable of all that could be offered: every State, and every Territory that aspires to become a State, will strive to keep the Indians as far as possible from its own borders; while powerful combinations of speculators will make their fight for the last acre of Indian lands with just as much rapacity as if they had not already, in Western phrase, "gobbled" a hundred thousand square miles of it.

In addition to the political, industrial, and speculative interests which will thus oppose the restoration of the policy of Indian seclusion from the shattered condition to which the events just recited have reduced it, three classes of persons may be counted on to lend their support to the plan of introducing the Indians, who have thus far been treated as "the wards of the nation," directly into the body of our citizenship. We have, first, those who have become impatient of the demands made upon the time of Congress and the attention of the people in the name of the Indians, and who wish, once for all, to have done with them. Such impatience is neither unnatural nor wholly unreasonable. It must be confessed that no good work ever made heavier drafts upon the faith and patience of the philanthropic. What with the triviality of the Indian character, the absurd punctilio with which, in his lowest estate, he insists on embarrassing the most ordinary business, and his devotion to sentiments utterly repugnant to our social and industrial genius; what, again, with the endless variety of tribal relations and tribal claims, and the complexity of tribal interests, aggravated by jealousy and suspicion where no previous intercourse has existed, and by feuds and traditions of hatred where intercourse has existed, — the conduct of Indian affairs, whether in legislation or in administration, is in no small degree perplexing and irritating. The Indian treaties prior to 1842 make up one entire volume of the General Statutes, while the treaties and Indian laws since that date would fill two volumes of equal size. It cannot be denied that this is taking a good deal of trouble for a very small and not very useful portion of the population of the country: and it is not to be wondered at that many citizens, and not a few Congressmen, are much disposed to cut the knot instead of untying it, and summarily dismiss the Indian as the subject of peculiar consideration, by enfranchising him, not for any good it may do to him, but for the relief of our legislation.

Next, we have that large and increasing class of Americans, who, either from natural bias, or from the severe political shocks of the last twelve years, have accepted what we may call the politics of despair, by which is meant, not so much a belief in any definite ill fortune for the Republic, as a conviction that the United States are being borne on to an end not seen, by a current which it is impossible to resist; that it is futile longer to seek to interpose restraints upon the rate of this progress, or to change its direction; that the nation has already gone far outside the traditional limits of safe political navigation, and is taking its course, for weal or woe, across an unknown sea, not unlike that little squadron which sailed out from the Straits of Saltez on the 3d of August, 1492. Many of the persons now holding these views were formerly among the most conservative of our people; but emancipation, negro suffrage, and the consolidation of power consequent upon the war, have wholly unsettled their convictions, leaving them either hopeless of the Republic, or, as temperament serves, eager to crowd on sail, and prove at once the worst and the best of fortune. In this despair of conservative methods, some of these men have acquired an oddly objective way of looking at their country, which to every man ought to be a part of himself, and have apparently as much of a curious as of a patriotic interest in watching the development of the new forms and forces of national life. Men of this class (and they are not few) are not likely to hesitate in extending to the Indians citizenship and the ballot. A little more or less, they think, can make no difference. After negro suffrage, any thing.

Finally, we have a class of persons, who, from no impatience of the subject, and from no indifference to the welfare of the aborigines, will oppose the policy of seclusion, as an anomaly not to be tolerated in our form of government. These are men who cannot bear, that, from any assumed necessity or for any supposed advantage, exception should be made of any class of inhabitants, or in respect to any portion of territory, to the rule of uniform rights and responsibilities, and of absolute freedom of movement, contract, and intercourse, the whole nation and the whole land over. Were the Indians ten times as numerous, were their claims to consideration stronger by no matter how much, and were the importance to them of seclusion far more clear than it appears, these political philosophers would steadily oppose the scheme. They might regret the mischiefs which would result to the Indian from exposure to corrupting influences; they might be disposed to favor the most liberal allowances from the public treasury, in compensation to him for his lands, and for his industrial endowment: but they would none the less relentlessly insist that the red man should take his equal chance with white and black, with all the privileges and all the responsibilities of political manhood.

In view of the likelihood that the expediency of Indian citizenship will thus become at an early date a practical legislative question, it seems desirable in the connection to state the constitutional relations of the subject. The judicial decisions are somewhat confused, although, from the date (1831) of the decision of Chief-Justice Marshall in the Cherokee Nation *vs.* the State of Georgia (5 Peters, 1), to that (1870) of the decision in the Cherokee Tobacco (11 Wallace, 616), there has been a marked progress (note especially the decision of Chief-Justice Taney in the United States *vs.* Rogers, 4 Howard, 567) towards the stronger affirmation of the complete and sufficient sovereignty of the United States. Yet in December, 1870, the Judiciary Committee of the Senate, Carpenter presenting the Report, after an incomplete, and in some respects an inaccurate and inconsequential * recital of judicial opinions, made the following startling announcement: —

* We are aware that this is a heavy charge; but it is justified by the facts. The recital is incomplete. The decision in the

"Inasmuch as the Constitution treats Indian tribes as belonging to the rank of nations capable of making treaties, it is evident that an act of Congress which should assume to treat the members of a tribe as subject to the municipal jurisdiction of the United States would be unconstitutional and void."

That this is not good law need not be argued, inasmuch as the decisions previously cited in the United States *vs.* Rogers and in the Cherokee Tobacco, assert the complete sovereignty of the United States in strong terms*; in the latter, the doctrine being explicitly affirmed, that not only

United States *vs.* Rogers is not referred to. This case is, as it was treated by the Supreme Court in the Cherokee Tobacco, of the highest importance.

The recital is inaccurate. An opinion is given at length as that of Kent in Jackson *vs.* Goodell, 20 Johnson, 193. This is a case in the Supreme Court of New York, Chief-Justice Spencer delivering the opinion, Kent having been previously appointed chancellor. The expressions quoted by the Committee are to be found in Goodell *vs.* Jackson, in error to the Court of Appeals, 20 Johnson, 693. The recital is inconsequential, as will appear by what is said further in the text.

* "We think it too firmly and clearly established to admit of dispute, that the Indian tribes residing within the territorial limits of the United States are subject to their authority; and where the country occupied by them is not within the limit of one of the States, Congress may by law punish any offence committed

does the capability of making a treaty with the United States, which has been held to reside in an Indian tribe, not exempt that tribe from the legislative power of Congress, but that not even a treaty made and ratified, among the stipulations of which is such an exemption, even were that exemption the consideration for cessions the benefit of which the United States has enjoyed and continues to enjoy, can hinder Congress from at any time extending its complete legislative control over the tribe. Considerations of good faith may influence individual Congressmen in such a case; but the constitutional competence of Congress in the premises is declared to be beyond question.

Nor is the extraordinary proposition of the Committee's report better in reason than in law. The argument is in effect this: The United States makes treaties with foreign nations; the United States cannot legislate for foreign nations; the United States may make treaties with Indian tribes: *ergo*,

there, whether the offender be a white man or an Indian."—*Taney, Chief-Justice.*

In the Cherokee Tobacco, the court, quoting from Chief-Justice Taney the sentence just preceding, and a similar utterance of Chief-Justice Marshall, remarks, "Both these propositions are so well settled in our jurisprudence, that it would be a waste of time to discuss them, or to refer to further authorities in their support."

the United States cannot legislate for Indian tribes. This course of reasoning implies that the sole objection to the United States legislating for foreign nations is, that they makes treaties with them: whereas there are several other good and sufficient objections thereto. It also implies that the sole consideration for the United States treating with Indian tribes, called by Chief-Justice Marshall "domestic dependent nations," is, that they cannot legislate for them: whereas the real consideration has been one of practical convenience, not of legislative competence.

We shall best set forth the constitutional relations of this subject by presenting the premises, whether of fact or of law, upon which all the judicial decisions relative thereto have been founded.

1. As matter of fact, the European powers engaged in the discovery and conquest of the New World left with the Indian tribes the regulation of their own domestic concerns, while claiming the sovereignty of the soil occupied by them. The Indian tribes thus continued to act as separate political communities.*

*Throughout the whole course of this discussion on the constitutional relations of the Indians, we should indicate as subject

2. The Constitution of the United States excludes from the basis of Congressional representation "Indians not taxed," without further defining the same.

3. The Congress of the United States has, with a few recent exceptions, treated Indians in tribal relations as without the municipal jurisdiction of the United States.

4. The Senate of the United States has confirmed nearly four hundred treaties, negotiated by the executive, under the general treaty-making powers conferred by the Constitution, with tribes which embrace about three-fifths of the present Indian population of the United States. The House of Representatives has, from the foundation of the government, as occasion required, originated bills for the appropriation of moneys to carry out the provisions of such treaties.

This comprises all that is essential in this connection. The *indicia* gathered from particular acts of the government, or from the phraseology

to possible exception the tribes found upon soil ceded by Mexico. It is claimed, that, as Mexico never treated the Indians within its jurisdiction other than as a peculiar class of citizens, all the members of those tribes became citizens of the United States by virtue of the provisions of the Treaty of Guadalupe Hidalgo, 1848.

of individual treaties, really add nothing to the above.

We believe the following propositions to be consistent with the facts of history and with the latest judicial decisions.

1. The exclusion by the Constitution of "Indians not taxed" from the basis of representation was in no sense a guaranty to the Indian tribes of their political autonomy, but was a provision in the interest of an equitable apportionment of political power among the States, some States having many Indians within their limits, others few or none.

2. The self-government enjoyed by the Indian tribes under the Constitution of the United States, as under the European powers, has always been a government by sufferance, by toleration, by permission. The United States, for their own convenience, have allowed this self-government, because to reduce the savages to the condition of submitting to civilized laws would have involved a great expense of blood and treasure; while through the tribal organization a much better government, for the purposes of the civilized power if not for the welfare of the Indians themselves, could be obtained, than through an administration which should disregard that organization. But this

toleration of savage self-government worked no prejudice to the sovereignty of the United States.

3. The decay of a tribe in numbers and in cohesion, no matter to what extent carried, does not bring the members of such tribe within the municipal jurisdiction of the State wherein they are found, so long as the tribal organization continues to be recognized by the National Government. See the Kansas Indians, 5 Wallace, 737.

4. Congress is constitutionally competent to extend the laws of the United States at once over every Indian tribe within the Territories, if not within the States of the Union, even though treaties may guarantee to individual tribes complete and perpetual political independence; the breach of faith involved in the latter case being matter for possible conscientious scruples on the part of legislators, not for judicial cognizance. See 11 Wallace, 616; 2 Curtis, 454; 1 Woolworth, 155.

We have thought it important thus to review the doctrine of the Report of the Senate Judiciary Committee, because, from the high standing of the Committee, from the assumption which the Report * makes of completeness in the citation of

* "Although the Committee have not regarded the questions proposed for their consideration by this resolution as at all diffi-

"treaties, laws, and judicial decisions" pertinent to the subject, on the express ground of a desire to enlighten, not only Congress, but the country, in respect to our Indian relations, and from the wide circulation given to the Report, as compared with that obtained by an ordinary decision of the Circuit or Supreme Court of the United States, the Report has apparently come to be accepted by Congress and the country as an authoritative exposition of the history and law of the subject; although, in the very month in which it was submitted to Congress, the Supreme Court, in the Cherokee Tobacco, pronounced a doctrine which cuts up that of the Report, root and branch.

Such being the constitutional competence of Congress to deal with the Indians, without re-

cult to answer, yet respect for the Senate, which ordered the investigation, and the existence of some loose popular notions of modern date in regard to the power of the President and Senate to exercise the treaty-making power in dealing with the Indian tribes, have induced your Committee to examine the questions thus at length, and present extracts from treaties, laws, and judicial decisions; and your Committee indulge the hope that a reference to these sources of information may tend to fix more clearly in the minds of Congress and the people the true theory of our relations to these unfortunate tribes."—*Report*, p. 11. It would, perhaps, have been fortunate had the Committee found the questions difficult.

straint either from the self-government hitherto permitted them, or from treaties to which the United States are a party, it is for Congress to decide, firstly, what the good faith of the nation requires, and, secondly, what course will best accomplish the social and industrial elevation of the native tribes, with due consideration had for the interests of the present body of citizens.

How, then, stands the matter with the faith of the nation? By the Report on Indian Affairs for 1872, there appear (p. 16) to be in the neighborhood of 120,000 Indians with whom the United States have no treaty relations. These certainly can have no claims to exemption from direct control, whenever the United States shall see fit to extend its laws over them, either to incorporate them in the body of its citizenship, or to seclude them for their own good. There are, again, as nearly as we can determine by a comparison of treaties with the Reports of the Indian Office, about 125,000 Indians with whom the United States have treaties unexpired, but to whom no distinct guaranty or promise of autonomy has been made. Examination of these treaties reveals nothing which should prevent the United States from establishing a magistracy and a code of laws for the government of these tribes, according to principles suited to their present condition, yet tending to raise them to a higher social and industrial condition. On the other hand, the perpetual interdiction of all white persons upon the reservations of these tribes, except "such officers, agents, and employees of the government as may be authorized to enter upon Indian reservations in discharge of duties enjoined by law," would seem to preclude the possibility of these regions ever being opened to settlement, and the Indians thereon resolved into the body of citizens on equal terms. But, as matter of fact, not even such treaty provisions need, with intelligent and firm but kindly management, greatly or long embarrass the government in the adjustment of the Indian question according to either principle which may be adopted, seclusion or citizenship. Few of these tribes but are obliged, even now, to seek from the United States more aid than they are entitled to by treaty; while it is certain that in the near future most, if not all, will be thrown in comparative helplessness upon our bounty. The United States being the sole party to which they can cede their lands (8 Wheaton, 543), and the sale of the great body of these lands being their only resource, the government will have the opportunity, not only without fraud or wrong to this people, but for their highest good, and indeed for their salvation from the doom otherwise awaiting them, to cancel the whole of these ill-considered treaties, leaving the natives where they ought to be, — subject to direct control by Congress. We repeat, there need never be any difficulty in securing, at the right time and in the right way, the relinquishment of lands or privileges from the Indians. They are, unfortunately, only too ready to sacrifice the future to present indulgence; while the government on its part can always afford to pay them far more for their lands than their lands are worth to them. Under this relation of the parties in interest, and with the pressure of actual want, due to the inability of the natives properly to cultivate what they possess, the United States may at an early date, with good faith and judicious management, easily secure the relinquishment of every franchise that stands in the way of a satisfactory adjustment of the difficulty.

There is still a third body of Indians, about 55,000 in number, occupying chiefly the regions known as the Indian Territory, and representing the tribes which were the subjects of the colonization policy of Pres. Monroe, to whom the United States have plighted their faith that no foreign authority shall ever be extended over them without their consent. These are not beggarly and vagabond Indians, to whom the offer of subsistence would be sufficient to obtain the relinquishment of their franchises, or the cession of their lands. They are self-supporting, independent, and even wealthy. Their cereal crops exceed those of all the Territories of the United States combined. In the number and value of horses and cattle, they are surpassed by the people of but one Territory; in expenditures for education, by the people of no Territory.* If these

* See Annual Report, Board of Indian Commissioners, 1872, p. 12.

Constant efforts are made to break the force of such comparisons as these, by asserting that the progress of the Indian Territory in industry and the arts of life is due to white men incorporated with the Creeks, Cherokees, and Choctaws. If this be true, it would seem that white men, when brought under Indian laws, and adopted into Indian families, exhibit qualities superior to those which they develop when controlling themselves, and organizing their own forms of industry and of government. This suggests the inquiry, whether it might not be well to turn over two or three Territories that might be named, to the Indians, with liberty to pick out white men for adoption and for instruction, in the hope that these communities might in time be brought up to the condition of that of which the Indians have had sole control for forty years.

people ever relinquish their autonomy, it will be because they desire the privileges of American citizens. This may well be in the immediate future, and surely will be, sooner or later, unless they are made to fear the violence and greed of their white neighbors. Meanwhile, they should be honorably protected in the enjoyment of their treaty rights. They have already advanced so far in civilization as to secure their own future, as against any thing but squatter and railroad rapacity; and their fate does not properly form a part of the Indian problem of the present day.

Excepting thus the present inhabitants of the so-called Indian Territory, who ought to be excepted from any scheme that embraces the half-civilized and the wholly savage tribes, we have practically a clear field for any policy which Congress shall determine to be best suited to the serious exigency of the situation; for, however easy to dismiss the subject for a time with ridicule, the task of so disposing a nomad population of 200,000 to 240,000, as to reduce to a minimum the obstruction it shall offer to the progress of settlement and of industry, without leaving the germs of lasting evil to a score of future States, and at the same time to secure the highest welfare of that population, — this task is a most serious one, to which the best statesmanship of the nation may well address itself.

In characterizing the classes of persons who will naturally be found among the advocates of the policy of an immediate bestowal of citizenship upon the Indian tribes, whether they be willing or unwilling, whether for good or evil, we have in effect stated all the arguments in favor of that policy; for it is not probable, that, aside from those who would properly be placed under one or another of the classes indicated, there are a score of persons reasonably well informed in Indian affairs, who would so much as affect to believe that such a course would have other than disastrous consequences to the natives.

The considerations which favor the policy of seclusion with more or less of industrial constraint are so direct and familiar, and are sustained by so general a concurrence of testimony and authority, that they will not require us greatly to protract this paper in their exposition and enforcement. These considerations are four in number; three of them having especial reference to the interests of the Indians, the fourth bearing on the welfare of the States to be formed out of the territory now roamed over by the native tribes.

First: so long as an Indian tribe is left to its own proper forces and dispositions, free from all foreign attraction, it is not only easily governed, but the whole body obeys the recognized law of the community with almost absolute unanimity. No expressions would be too strong to characterize the social homogeneity of an Indian tribe, and the complete domination of the accepted ideas of right and wrong, of honor and baseness. Public opinion is there conclusive upon every individual; and the spectacle, seen in every town and village with us, of large numbers openly practising that which public opinion reprobates, or refusing to do that which public opinion prescribes, is wholly unknown. We do not say that this is the most desirable as the ultimate form of society; but this tyranny of sentiment may and should be made a most powerful auxiliary for good in the early stages of industrial and social progress for this people.

Second: it is unfortunately true, that, when the Indian is, by the powerful attraction of a race which his savage breast never fails to recognize as superior, released from the control of the public sentiment which he has been accustomed to obey, he submits himself by an almost irresistible tendency to the worst and not to the best influences of civilized society. While there are undeniably exceptions to this statement, it is supported by such a mass of melancholy evidence in the history of scores of tribes once renowned for all the native virtues, that no one has the right to advocate the introduction to such influences of uninstructed and unprovided tribes, unless he is prepared to contemplate the ruin of nine-tenths of the subjects of his policy.

Nor is it the worst elements of the Indian which thus submit themselves to the worst elements of the white community. The very men who bear themselves most loftily, according to the native standards of virtue, are quite as likely to fall, under exposure to white contact, as are the weakest of the tribe. Their familiar attractions all broken, their immemorial traditions rudely dispelled, their natural leadership destroyed, the members of a wild tribe, strong and weak together, become the easy prey of the rascally influences of civilized society.

Third: the experiment of citizenship, except with the more advanced tribes, is at the serious risk, amounting almost to a certainty, of the immediate loss to the Indians of the whole of their scanty patrimony, through the improvident and wasteful alienation of the lands patented to them, the Indians being left thus without resource for the future, except in the bounty of the general government or in local charity. On this point a few facts will be more eloquent than many words.

The United States have by recent treaties or legislative enactments admitted to citizenship the following Indians, — In Kansas, Kickapoos, 12; Delawares, 20; Wyandots, 473; Pottawatomies, 1,604: in Dakota, Sioux, 250: in Minnesota, Winnebagoes, 159: in Wisconsin, Stockbridges, to a number not yet officially ascertained: in Michigan, Ottawas and Chippewas, 6,039: in the Indian Territory, Ottawas of Blanchard's Fork, 150. Time has not yet been given for the full development of the consequences of thus devolving responsibility upon these Indians; but we already have information, official or semi-official, to the effect that the majority of the Pottawatomie citizens, after selling their lands in Kansas, have gone to the Indian Territory, and re-associated themselves as a tribe; that of the Wyandots, considerable numbers have attached themselves to the re-organized tribe in the Indian Territory; that of the citizen Ottawas of Blanchard's Fork, nearly all have disposed of their allotted lands, and are still cared for to some extent by the government as Indians; that of the Ottawas and Chippewas of Michigan, a majority certainly, and probably a large majority, have sold the lands patented to them in severalty, — in many cases the negotiation preceding the issue of patents, two parties of white sharpers contesting for the favor of the agent, in the way of early information as to the precise lands assigned, and the disappointed faction, in at least one instance, resorting to burglary and larceny for the needed documents.

It will be thus seen, that, of these Indians upon whom the experiment of citizenship has been tried, more than half, probably at least two-thirds, are now homeless, and must be re-endowed by the government, or they will sink to a condition of hopeless poverty and misery.

Fourth: the dissolution of the tribal bonds, and the dispersing of two hundred thousand Indians among the settlements, will devolve upon the present and future States beyond the Missouri an almost intolerable burden of vagabondage, pauperism, and crime. It is not even essential to the result of a dispersion of these tribes that the law should pronounce their dissolution as political communities. Unless the system of reservations shall soon be recast, and the laws of non-intercourse thoroughly enforced, the next fifteen or twenty years will see the great majority of the Indians on the plains mixed up with white settlements, wandering in small camps from place to place, shifting sores upon the public body, the men resorting for a living to basket-making, beggary, and hog-stealing, the women to fortune-telling, beggary, and harlotry; while a remnant will seek to maintain a little longer, in the mountains, their savage independence, fleeing before the advance of settlement when they can, fighting in sullen despair when they must. It is doubtless true that some tribes could still remain together as social, even after being dissolved as legal, communities; but the fate we have indicated would certainly befall by far the greater part of the Indians of the plains, were the reservation system broken up in their present social and industrial condition. To believe that a pioneer population of two, three, or four millions, such as is likely to occupy this region within the next twenty years, can, in addition to its own proper elements of disorder, safely absorb such a mass of corruption, requires no small faith in the robust virtue of our people, and in the saving efficacy of republican institutions.

This last consideration we have urged, not on behalf of the Indians, but in the interest of the present white communities beyond the Missouri, to whom such a dispersion of the tribes would be a far greater burden than the maintenance of the reservation system in its integrity could possibly be, and in the interest of a score of States of the Union yet to be formed out of that territory. Surely it is not in such cement that we wish to have the foundations of our future society laid.

We conclude, then, that Indian citizenship is to be regarded as an end, and not as a means; that it is the goal to which each tribe should in turn be conducted, through a course of industrial instruction and constraint, maintained by the government with kindness but also with firmness, under the shield of the reservation system. It is true that this system can no longer be kept up without sacrifice on our part. In the days of Pres. Monroe, the sequestration of the Indians involved only the expense of transporting eighty or ninety thousand persons to a region not settled, nor then desired for settlement. To-day there is no portion of our territory where citizens of the United States are not preparing to make their homes. To cut off a reservation sufficient for the wants of this unfortunate people in their rude ways of life; to hedge it in with strict laws of non-intercourse, turning aside, for the purpose, railway and highway alike; and, upon the soil thus secluded, to work patiently out the problem of Indian civilization, — is not to be deemed a light sacrifice to national honor and duty. Yet that the government and people of the United States cannot discharge their obligations to the aborigines without pains and care and expense, affords no reason for declining the task.

The claim of the Indian upon us is of no common character. The advance of railways and settlements is fast pushing him from his home, and, in the steady extinction of game, is cutting him off from the only means of subsistence of which he knows how to avail himself. He will soon be left homeless and helpless in the midst of civilization, upon the soil that once was his alone. The freedom of territorial and industrial expansion which is bringing imperial greatness to the nation, to the Indian brings wretchedness, destitution, beggary. Surely there is obligation found, in such considerations as these, to make good in some way to him the loss by which we so largely gain. Nor is this obligation one that can be discharged by lavish endowments, which it is of moral certainty he will squander, or by merely placing him in situations where he might prosper, had he the industrial aptitudes of the white man, acquired through centuries of laborious training. Savage as he is by no fault of his own, and stripped at once of savage independence and savage competence by our act, for our advantage, we have made ourselves responsible before God and the world for his rescue from destruction, and his elevation to social and industrial manhood, at whatever expense and at whatever inconvenience. The corner-stone of our Indian policy should be the recognition by government and by the people, that we owe the Indian, not endowments and lands only, but also forbearance, patience, care, and instruction.

It is not unusual to sneer at the sentimentality of "the Quakers" and other active friends of this race. But we may as well remember that posterity will grow much more sentimental over the fate of the Indian than any Quaker or philanthropist of to-day. The United States will be judged at the bar of history according to what they shall have done in two respects, — by their disposition of negro slavery, and by their treatment of the Indians. In the one matter, the result is fortunately secure; nor will it be remembered against us, in diminution of our honor, that we procrastinated and sought to evade the issue, and for a time made terms and compromised with wrong. In that, when at last we were brought face to face with the question, we did the one thing that was right, and in tears and blood expiated our own and our fathers' errors, the ages to come will give us no grudging and stinted praise. Would that we were equally sure that no stain will rest upon our fame for what shall yet be done or left undone towards the original possessors of our soil! What is past cannot be recalled; nor has any thing yet gone into history that need deeply dishonor us as a nation. Posterity will judge very leniently of all that has been done in heat of blood, in the struggle for life and for the possession of the soil by the early Colonists; it will not greatly attribute blame that, in our industrial and territorial expansion, and a conquest of savage nature more rapid than is recorded of any other people, savage man has suffered somewhat at our hands; it will not attempt nicely to apportion the mutual injuries of the frontier, to decide which was first and which was worst in wrong, red man or white; it will have ample consideration for the difficulties which the government has encountered in preserving the peace between the natives and the bold, rude pioneers of civilization. But if, when the Indians shall have been thrown helpless upon our mercy, surrounded and disarmed by the extension of settlement, and impoverished by the very causes which promote our wealth and greatness, we fail to make ample provision out of our abundance, and to apply it in all patience and with all pains, to save alive these remnants of a once powerful people, and reconcile them to civilization, there is much reason to fear, that, however successfully we may excuse ourselves to ourselves by pleading the manifest destiny of the Anglo-Saxon race, impartial history will pronounce us recreant to a sacred duty.

AN ACCOUNT

OF THE NUMBERS, LOCATION, AND SOCIAL, AND INDUSTRIAL CONDITION OF EACH IMPORTANT TRIBE AND BAND OF INDIANS WITHIN THE UNITED STATES.

[From the report of Francis A. Walker, U. S. Commissioner of Indian Affairs, for the year 1872.]

THE Indians within the limits of the United States, exclusive of those in Alaska, number, approximately, 300,000.

(*a*) They may be divided, according to their geographical location or range, into five grand divisions, as follows: in Minnesota, and States east of the Mississippi River, about 32,500; in Nebraska, Kansas, and the Indian Territory, 70,650; in the Territories of Dakota, Montana, Wyoming, and Idaho, 65,000; in Nevada, and the Territories of Colorado, New Mexico, Utah, and Arizona, 84,000; and on the Pacific slope, 48,000.

(*b*) In respect to the three lines of railroads—built or projected—between the States and the Pacific Ocean, viz., the northern, central, and southern routes, they may be divided, excluding those residing east of Minnesota and of the Missouri River south of Dakota, as follows: between the proposed northern route and the British Possessions, about 36,000; between the northern and central routes, 92,000; between the central and the proposed southern routes, 61,000; and between the southern route and Mexico, 85,000: making a total of 274,000.

(*c*) As regards their means of support and methods of subsistence, they may be divided as follows: those who support themselves upon their own reservations, receiving nothing from the government except interest on their own moneys, or annuities granted them in consideration of the cession of their lands to the United States, number about 130,000; those who are entirely subsisted by the government, about 31,000; those in part subsisted, 84,000,—together about 115,000; those who subsist by hunting and fishing, upon roots, nuts, berries, &c., or by begging and stealing, about 55,000.

(*d*) They may be divided again, with respect

to their connection with the government, as follows: there are about 150,000 who may be said to remain constantly upon their reservations, and are under the complete control of agents appointed by the government; 95,000 who at times visit their agencies either for food or for gossip, or for both, but are generally roaming either on or off their reservations, engaged in hunting or fishing; and 55,000 who never visit an agency, and over whom the government as yet exercises practically no control, but most of whom are inoffensive, and commit no acts of hostility against the government.

(*e*) Again: it may be said, that, of the 300,000 Indians of the country, about 180,000 have treaties with the government; 40,000 have no treaties with the United States, but have reservations set apart by executive order or otherwise for their occupancy, and are in charge of agents appointed by the government; 25,000 have no reservations, but are more or less under the control of agents appointed for them, and receive more or less assistance from the government; the remainder consisting of the same 55,000 already twice described, over whom the government exercises, practically, no control, and for whom there are no treaty or other provisions.

(*f*) As to civilization, they may, though with no great degree of assurance, be divided, according to a standard taken with reasonable reference to what might fairly be expected of a race with such antecedents and traditions, as follows: civilized, 97,000; semi-civilized, 125,000; wholly barbarous, 78,000.

MINNESOTA, AND EAST OF THE MISSISSIPPI RIVER.

NEW YORK.

The Indians of New York, remnants of the once powerful "Six Nations," number five thousand and seventy. They occupy six reservations in the State, containing in the aggregate 68,668 acres. Two of these reservations, viz., the Alleghany and Cattaraugus, belonged originally to the Colony of Massachusetts, but by sale and assignment passed into the hands of a company, the Indians holding a perpetual right of occupancy, and the company referred to, or the individual members thereof, owning the ultimate fee. The same state of facts formerly existed in regard to the Tonawanda reserve; but the Indians who occupy it have purchased the ultimate fee of a portion of the reserve, which is now held in trust for them by the Secretary of the Interior. The State of New York exercises sovereignty over these reservations. The reservations occupied by the Oneidas, Onondagas, and Tuscaroras, have been provided for by treaty stipulations between the Indians and the State of New York. All six reserves are held and occupied by the Indians in common. While the Indian tribes of the continent, with few exceptions, have been steadily decreasing in numbers, those of New York have of late more than held their own, as is shown by an increase of one hundred in the present reports over the reported number in 1871, and of thirteen hundred over the number embraced in the United-States census of 1860. On the New-York reservations are twenty-eight schools; the attendance during some portions of the past year exceeding eleven hundred, the daily average attendance being six hundred and eight. Of the teachers employed, fifteen are Indians, as fully competent for this position as their white associates. An indication of what is to be accomplished in the future, in an educational point of view, is found in the successful effort made in August last to establish a teacher's institute on the Cattaraugus reservation for the education of teachers specially for Indian schools. Thirty-eight applicants attended; and twenty-six are now under training.

The statistics of individual wealth and of the aggregate product of agricultural and other industry are, in general, favorable; and a considerable increase in these regards is observed from year to year. Twenty thousand acres are under cultivation: the cereal crops are good; while noticeable success has been achieved in the raising of fruit.

MICHIGAN.

The bands or tribes residing in Michigan are the Chippewas of Saginaw, Swan Creek, and Black River; the Ottawas and Chippewas; the Pottawatomies of Huron; and the L'Anse band of Chippewas.

The Chippewas of Saginaw, Swan Creek, and Black River, numbering sixteen hundred and thirty, and the Ottawas and Chippewas, six thousand and thirty-nine, are indigenous to the country. They are well advanced in civilization; have, with few exceptions, been allotted lands under treaty provisions, for which they have received patents; and are now entitled to all the privileges and benefits of citizens of the United States. Those to whom no allotments have been made can secure homesteads under the provisions of the act of June 10, 1872. All treaty stipulations with these Indians have expired. They now have no money or other annuities paid to them by the United States Government. The three tribes first named have in all four schools, with one hundred and fifteen scholars; and the last, two schools, with one hundred and fifty-two scholars.

The Pottawatomies of Huron number about fifty.

The L'Anse band of Chippewas, numbering eleven hundred and ninety-five, belong with the other bands of the Chippewas of Lake Superior. They occupy a reservation of about forty-eight thousand three hundred acres, situated on Lake Superior, in the extreme northern part of the State. But few of them are engaged in agriculture, most of them depending for their subsistence on hunting and fishing. They have two schools, with an attendance of fifty-six scholars.

The progress of the Indians of Michigan in civilization and industry has been greatly hindered in the past by a feeling of uncertainty in regard to their permanent possession and enjoyment of their homes. Since the allotment of land, and the distribution of either patents or homestead certificates to these Indians (the L'Anse or Lake

Superior Chippewas, a people of hunting and fishing habits, excepted), a marked improvement has been manifested on their part in regard to breaking land and building houses. The aggregate quantity of land cultivated by the several tribes is eleven thousand six hundred and twenty acres; corn, oats, and wheat being the chief products. The dwellings occupied consist of two hundred and forty-four frame and eight hundred and thirty-five log houses. The aggregate population of the several tribes named (including the confederated "Chippewas, Ottawas, and Pottawatomies," about two hundred and fifty souls, with whom the government made a final settlement in 1866 of its treaty obligations) is, by the report of their agent for the current year, nine thousand one hundred and seventeen, — an increase over the number reported for 1871 of four hundred and two, due, however, perhaps as much to the return of absent Indians as to the excess of births over deaths. In educational matters these Indians have, of late, most unfortunately, fallen short of the results of former years; for the reason mainly that, their treaties expiring, the provisions previously existing for educational uses failed.

WISCONSIN.

The bands or tribes in Wisconsin are the Chippewas of Lake Superior, the Menomonees, the Stockbridges and Munsees, the Oneidas, and certain stray bands (so called) of Winnebagoes, Pottawatomies, and Chippewas.

The Chippewas of Lake Superior (under which head are included the following bands: Fond du Lac, Boise Forte, Grand Portage, Red Cliff, Bad River, Lac de Flambeau, and Lac Court D'Oreille) number about five thousand one hundred and fifty. They constitute a part of the Ojibways (anglicized in the term Chippewas), formerly one of the most powerful and warlike nations in the north-west, embracing many bands, and ranging over an immense territory, extending along the shores of Lakes Huron, Michigan, and Superior, to the steppes of the Upper Mississippi. Of this great nation large numbers are still found in Minnesota, many in Michigan, and a fragment in Kansas.

The bands above mentioned by name are at present located on several small reservations set apart for them by treaties of Sept. 30, 1854, and April 7, 1866, in Wisconsin and Minnesota, comprising in all about six hundred and ninety-five thousand two hundred and ninety acres. By act of Congress of May 29, 1872, provision was made for the sale, with the consent of the Indians, of three of these reservations, viz., the Lac de Flambeau and Lac Court D'Oreille in Wisconsin, and the Fond du Lac in Minnesota; and for the removal of the Indians located thereon to the Bad River reservation, where there is plenty of good, arable land, and where they can be properly cared for, and instructed in agriculture and mechanics.

The greater part of these Indians at present lead a somewhat roving life, finding their subsistence chiefly in game hunted by them, in the rice gathered in its wild state, and in the fish afforded by waters conveniently near. Comparatively little is done in the way of cultivating the soil. Certain bands have of late been greatly demoralized by contact with persons employed in the construction of the Northern Pacific Railroad, the line of which runs near one (the Fond du Lac) of their reservations. Portions of this people, however, especially those situated at the Bad River reservation, have begun to evince an earnest desire for self-improvement. Many live in houses of rude construction, and raise small

crops of grain and vegetables; others labor among the whites; and a number find employment in cutting rails, fence-posts, and saw-logs for the government. In regard to the efforts made to instruct the children in letters, it may be said, that, without being altogether fruitless, the results have been thus far meagre and somewhat discouraging. The majority of the parents profess to wish to have their children educated, and ask for schools; but, when the means are provided and the work undertaken, the difficulties in the way of success to any considerable extent appear in the undisciplined character of the scholars, which has to be overcome by the teacher without parental co-operation, and in the great irregularity of attendance at school, especially on the part of those who are obliged to accompany their parents to the rice-fields, the sugar-camps, or the fishing-grounds.

The Menomonees number thirteen hundred and sixty-two, and are located on a reservation of two hundred and thirty thousand four hundred acres in the north-eastern part of Wisconsin. They formerly owned most of the eastern portion of the State, and, by treaty entered into with the government on the 18th October, 1848, ceded the same for a home in Minnesota upon lands that

had been obtained by the United States from the Chippewas; but, becoming dissatisfied with the arrangement, as not having accorded them what they claimed to be rightfully due, subsequently protested, and manifested great unwillingness to remove. In view of this condition of affairs, they were, by the President, permitted to remain in Wisconsin, and temporarily located upon the lands they now occupy, which were secured to them by a subsequent treaty made with the tribe on the 12th May, 1854. This reservation is well watered by lakes and streams, the latter affording excellent power and facilities for moving logs and lumber to market; the most of their country abounding with valuable pine timber. A considerable portion of the Menomonees have made real and substantial advancement in civilization; numbers of them are engaged in agriculture; others find remunerative employment in the lumbering camp established upon their reservation, under the management of the government agent, while a few still return, at times, to their old pursuits of hunting and fishing.

Under the plan adopted by the department in 1871, in regard to cutting and selling the pine timber belonging to these Indians, 2,000,000 feet have been cut and driven, realizing $23,731, of which individual Indians received for their labor over $3,000, the treasury of the tribe deriving a net profit of $5 per thousand feet. The agent estimates, that, for labor done by the Indians upon the reservation, at lumbering, and for work outside on railroads, during the past year, about twenty thousand dollars has been earned and received, exclusive of the labor rendered in building houses, raising crops, making sugar, gathering rice, and hunting for peltries. The work of education upon the reservations has been of late quite unsatisfactory, but one small school being now in operation, with seventy scholars, the average attendance being fifty.

The Stockbridges and Munsees, numbering two hundred and fifty, occupy a reservation of sixty thousand eight hundred acres adjoining the Menomonees. The Stockbridges came originally from Massachusetts and New York. After several removals they, with the Munsees, finally located on their present reservation. Under the provisions of the act of Feb. 6, 1871, steps are now being taken to dispose of all of their reservation, with the exception of eighteen sections best adapted for agricultural purposes, which are reserved for their future use. They have no treaty stipulations with the United States at the present time; nor do they receive any annuities of any kind from the government. These tribes — indeed, it may be said this tribe (the Stockbridges); for of the Munsees there probably remain not more than a half a dozen souls — were formerly an intelligent, prosperous people, not a whit behind the most advanced of the race, possessed of good farms, well instructed, and industrious. Unfortunately for them, though much to the advantage of the government, which acquired thereby a valuable tract of country for white settlement, they removed, in 1857, to their present place of abode. The change has proved highly detrimental to their interests and prospects. Their new reservation, the greater part poor in soil and seriously affected by wet seasons and frequent frosts, has never yielded them more than a meagre subsistence. Many have for this reason left the tribe, and have been for years endeavoring to obtain a livelihood among the whites, maintaining but little intercourse with those remaining on the reservation, yet still holding their rights in the tribal property. The result has been bickerings and faction quarrels, prejudicial to the peace and advancement of the community. More than one-half of the present membership of the tribe, from both the "citizen" and the "Indian" parties, into which it has been long divided, are reported by the agent as having decided to avail themselves of the enrollment provisions in the act of Congress of February, 1871, before referred to, by which they will finally receive their share of the tribal property, and become citizens of the United States. Those who desire to retain their tribal relation under the protection of the United States may, under the act adverted to, if they so elect by their council, procure a new location for their future home. The school interests and religious care of this people are under the superintendence of Mr. Jeremiah Slingerland, a Stockbridge of much repute for his intelligence, and his success in the cause of the moral and educational improvement of his people.

The Oneidas, numbering twelve hundred and fifty-nine, have a reservation of 60,800 acres near Green Bay. They constitute the greater portion of the tribe of that name (derived from Lake Oneida, where the tribe then resided), formerly one of the "Six Nations." Two hundred and fifty of the Oneidas yet remain in New York on the reservations already described. Those who are found in Michigan are progressing in the arts of civilized life, many of them being intelligent, industrious, and ripe for citizenship. The progress of those best disposed and most advanced is, however, retarded by the fact of the tribal lands being held in common, by which the incentive to individual exertion is greatly impaired, and habits of industry and frugality discouraged. There are also some members who fail to keep pace with the progress of the tribe, in part, probably, from the same cause which hinders the improvement of those better disposed, but principally from that fatal curse of the Indian, the passion for intoxicating liquor, which is especially developed among those members of the tribe who are engaged in lumbering.

It is now believed that a large majority of the tribe favor the division of their lands, and the allotment of parcels to families and individuals, — a measure deemed to be of the first importance to the future welfare of this people, and which, it is suggested, should be the subject of legislative action with a view to its consummation at the earliest practicable date. There are two schools for this tribe, having on the rolls two hundred and seventeen scholars, the average attendance being ninety.

The stray bands of Winnebagoes, Chippewas, and Pottawatomies number about sixteen hundred. They are scattered in small parties over the central and northern portions of the State, and are those members of the tribes named who did not remove when their respective tribes went west of the Mississippi. They receive no assistance from the government, and subsist by cultivating small patches of corn and vegetables, by hunting, fishing, and gathering berries, and by working for the whites at certain seasons of the year. A number own a few acres: others rent small patches from the whites. They are accused of causing considerable annoyance to the farmers in some localities; and, on account of complaints having been made in this respect, Congress has appropriated funds to remove them to the tribes to which they respectively belong, or to some place in the Indian Territory south of Kansas. For various reasons their removal has not yet been undertaken. Indeed, while this may be found practicable, I doubt whether it can be thoroughly accomplished without additional and severe legislation on the part of Congress, as the Indians are attached to the country, and express great repugnance to their contemplated removal from it. On this account, and for the reason that they cannot be supposed to feel much interest in those from whom they have been so long separated, and by whom they might not be heartily welcomed, it is probable that those who should be removed against their will would return to their old haunts, and do the same as often as they should be removed therefrom.

MINNESOTA.

The Indians residing within the limits of Minnesota, as in the case of those of the same name living in Wisconsin, heretofore noticed, constitute a portion of the Ojibway or Chippewa nation, and comprise the following bands: Mississippi, Pillager, Winnebagoshish, Pembina, Red Lake, Boise Forte, Fond du Lac, and Grand Portage. The last three bands, being attached to the agency for the Chippewas of Lake Superior, have been treated of in connection with the Indians of Wisconsin. The five first-named bands number in the aggregate about six thousand four hundred and fifty-five souls, and occupy, or rather it is intended they shall ultimately occupy, ample reservations in the central and northern portion of the State, known as the White Earth, Leech Lake, and Red Lake reservations, containing altogether about 4,672,000 acres, a portion of which is very valuable for its pine timber.

The condition of these Indians, except those upon the White Earth reservation, has been but little changed during the past year from that of several years preceding. Great difficulty is still experienced in inducing the Indians to remain permanently upon their reservations. A roving life is still preferred by many, their old haunts presenting more attractions for them than new homes with the unavoidable necessity of labor for subsistence. Yet no inconsiderable number are already evidencing by their efforts, as well as by their professions, a new spirit of industry and enterprise. The past year has been one of trouble and unusual excitement on the part of both whites and Indians, on account of the ill behavior of the Pillager band; and apprehensions of a serious outbreak were for a time entertained. Nine murders of citizens are reported to have been committed by individual Chippewas, mainly if not wholly of this band; and threats were made on the part of some of the

Pillagers, which, if carried out, would have involved nearly all of the Indians of this section in hostilities. Happily, by the prompt arrival of United States troops upon the White Earth reservation, and more especially by the strong disapprobation of the conduct of the Pillagers expressed in council by the general body of Leech Lake Indians, and their evident purpose to unite with the government in putting down any and all enemies of the peace, the crisis was passed; and comparative quiet has again been restored. In view of the atrocities committed by the Pillagers, and of the alarm occasioned thereby among the citizens of Minnesota, Gov. Austin issued a proclamation requiring all Indians to remain upon their reservations under penalty of arrest, to be effected by the militia of the State, should it be found necessary. In the present condition of things, however, a compliance by all with this requirement is simply impossible; and there is danger, that, without the exercise of great prudence and forbearance on the part of the State authorities, further and greater difficulties may arise. The "Otter Tail" Pillagers, to whom the difficulties referred to are principally due, have the right to a home on the White Earth reservation.

They removed to it in 1871; but, as they were not provided with the means of opening farms, nor with subsistence during the time necessary to raise a crop, they returned to their former haunts. They are now warned off from their grounds at Otter Tail by the State authorities. The larger portion of the Pillagers, together with the Winnebagoshish band, about fifteen hundred in number, live around Leech Lake. Their general reputation for turbulence and worthlessness of character is well known and of long standing: still there are those who seem willing and ready to work if assisted by the government.

Agent Smith, in charge, says that their country is barren, with only here and there patches susceptible of tillage, accessible only by canoe or steamboat. In this connection, and adverting to the murders committed by the Pillagers, it is but just to notice that all lawlessness in Minnesota, in the region of the Indian reservations, is not confined to Indians. The murder of two Indians of the Otter Tail Pillagers, for the offence of camping on a white man's ground, is reported; while two others, who had been arrested at White Earth on suspicion of complicity in a murder, and lodged in jail for trial, were taken therefrom by a mob, and hung. Such conduct can but have a pernicious effect upon the Indian mind, and tend to arouse a spirit of revenge and retaliation.

Mississippi bands. — These Indians reside in different localities. Most of them are on their reservation at White Earth: others are at Mille Lac, Gull Lake, and some at White Oak Point reservations. Upon the first-named reservation operations have been quite extensive in the erection of school-buildings, dwelling-houses, shops, and mills, and in breaking ground. At one time during the past summer there was a prospect of an abundant yield from 300 acres sown in cereals; but, unfortunately, the grasshoppers swept away the entire crop; and a second crop of buckwheat and turnips proved a failure. The Indians on this reservation are well-behaved, and inclined to be industrious. Many of them are engaged in tilling the soil, while others are learning the mechanical arts; and they may, as a body, be said to be making considerable progress in the pursuits of civilized life. About one-half of the Indians at Gull Lake have been removed to White Earth: the remainder are opposed to removal, and will, in their present feeling, rather forfeit their annuities than change their location. The Mille Lac

Chippewas, who continue to occupy the lands ceded by them in 1863, with reservation of the right to live thereon during good behavior, are indisposed to leave their old home for the new one designed for them on the White Earth reservation. Only about twenty-five have thus far been induced to remove. Their present reservation is rich in pine lands, the envy of lumber dealers; and there is a strong pressure on all sides for their early removal. They should have help from the government, whether they remain or remove; and this could be afforded to a sufficient extent by the sale for their benefit of the timber upon the lands now occupied by them. Probably the government could provide for them in no better way.

The White Oak Point Chippewas were formerly known as Sandy Lake Indians. They were removed in 1867 from Sandy Lake and Rabbit Lake to White Oak Point on the Mississippi, near the eastern part of the Leech Lake reservation. This location is unfavorable to their moral improvement and material progress, from its proximity to the lumber-camps of the whites. Thus far the effort made to better their condition, by placing them on farming land, has proved a failure. The ground broken for them has gone back into grass; and their log-houses are in ruin, the former occupants betaking themselves to their wonted haunts. It would be well if these Indians could be induced to remove to the White Earth reservation.

At Red Lake the Indians have had a prosperous year: good crops of corn and potatoes have been raised, and a number of houses built. This band would be in much better circumstances were they possessed of a greater quantity of arable lands. That to which they are at present limited allows but five acres, suitable for that use, to each family. It is proposed to sell their timber, and with the proceeds clear lands, purchase stock, and establish a manual-labor school.

The Pembina bands reside in Dakota Territory, but are here noticed in connection with the Minnesota Indians, because of their being attached to the same agency. They have no reservation, having ceded their lands by treaty made in 1863, but claim title to Turtle Mountain in Dakota, on which some of them resided at the time of the treaty, and which lies west of the line of the cession then made. They number, the full-bloods about three hundred and fifty, and the half-breeds about one hundred. They lead a somewhat nomadic life, depending upon the chase for a precarious subsistence, in connection with an annuity from the government of the United States.

The Chippewas of Minnesota have had but few educational advantages; but with the facilities now being afforded, and with the earnest endeavors that are now being put forth by their agent and the teachers employed, especially at White Earth, it is expected that their interests in this regard will be greatly promoted. At White Earth school operations have been quite successful; so much so, that it will require additional accommodations to meet the demands of the Indians for the education of their children. The only other school in operation is that at Red Lake, under the auspices of the American Indian Mission Association.

INDIANA.

There are now in Indiana about three hundred and forty-five Miamies, who did not go to Kansas when the tribe moved to that section under the treaty of 1840. They are good citizens, many being thrifty farmers, giving no trouble either to their white neighbors or to the government. There is also a small band called the Eel River band of Miamies, residing in this State and in Michigan.

NORTH CAROLINA, TENNESSEE, AND GEORGIA.

Cherokees.—There are residing in these States probably about seventeen hundred Cherokees, who elected to remain, under the provisions respecting Cherokees averse to removal, contained in the twelfth article of the treaty with the Cherokees of 1835. Under the act of July 29, 1848, a *per capita* transportation and subsistence fund of $53.33 was created and set apart for their benefit in accordance with a census-roll made under the provisions of said act, the interest on which fund until such time as they shall individually remove to the Indian country is the only money to which those named in said roll, who are living, or the heirs of those who have deceased, are entitled. This interest is too small to be of any benefit; and some action should be taken by Congress, with a view of having all business matters between these Indians and the government settled, by removing such of them west as now desire to go, and paying those who decline to remove the *per capita* fund referred to. The government has no agent residing with these Indians. In accordance with their earnestly expressed desire to be brought under the immediate charge of the government, as its wards,

Congress, by law approved July 27, 1868, directed that the Secretary of the Interior should cause the Commissioner of Indian Affairs to take the same supervisory charge of them as of other tribes of Indians; but this practically amounts to nothing, in the absence of means to carry out the intention of the law with any beneficial result to the Indians. The condition of this people is represented to be deplorable. Before the late rebellion they were living in good circumstances, engaged, with all the success which could be expected, in farming, and in various minor industrial pursuits. Like all other inhabitants of this section, they suffered much during the war, and are now from this and other causes much impoverished.

FLORIDA.

Seminoles. — There are a few Seminoles — supposed to number about three hundred — still residing in Florida, being those, or the descendants of those, who refused to accompany the tribe when it removed to the west many years ago. But little is known of their condition and temper.

NEBRASKA, KANSAS, AND THE INDIAN TERRITORY.

The tribes residing in Nebraska, Kansas, and the Indian Territory are divided as follows: in Nebraska about 6,485; in Kansas, 1,500; in the Indian Territory, 62,465.

NEBRASKA.

The Indians in Nebraska are the Santee Sioux, Winnebagoes, Omahas, Pawnees, Sacs and Foxes of the Missouri, Iowas, and the Otoes and Missourias.

The Santee Sioux, now numbering nine hundred and sixty-five, a decrease from last year of twenty-two, are a portion of the Sisseton, Wahpeton, Medawakanton, and Wahpakoota bands of Sioux of the Mississippi, belonging thus to the great Sioux or Dakota nation. They formerly, with other members of the same bands, — now located on reservations in Dakota, one at Devil's Lake in the north-east corner of the Territory, and another at Lake Traverse near their old home, — had an extensive and valuable reservation in Minnesota, stretching, with a width of ten miles, a long distance on the south side of the Minnesota River;

and were comparatively wealthy and prosperous until the Sioux outbreak in 1862, in which, it will be remembered, nearly one thousand white citizens lost their lives. After the suppression of hostilities consequent on this outbreak, most of the Santee Sioux were removed, in 1863, to the Crow Creek reservation, and finally, in 1866, to their present location near the mouth of the Niobrara River, at which point their numbers were increased, to the extent of about two hundred, by the accession of other Sioux, who had been held at Davenport, Io., as prisoners, charged with complicity in the outbreak, but were pardoned by the President.

The reservation of the Santee Sioux contains 83,200 acres; of which a small portion only is suitable for agricultural purposes, the country generally being broken with high bluffs and deep ravines. Lands have been allotted in severalty to over two hundred. These Indians are peaceable, industrious, and well advanced in the arts of life, and will soon render themselves independent of the assistance now afforded by the government. They have about five hundred acres in cultivation; upon which good crops of wheat, corn, oats, potatoes, &c., are raised, when not destroyed by that scourge of the country, the grasshopper. The houses of the Santee Sioux are generally of rude structure; those first built being without windows, and having only dirt floors and roofs. The Indians are, however, improving of late in this regard, and building much more durable and comfortable dwellings. They are parties to the treaty made in 1868 with the nine bands of the Sioux nation, ranging in the region of the Upper Missouri River. In addition to the benefits derived by the Santee Sioux under this treaty, they have moneys resulting from the sale of their lands in Minnesota, which are being used for their benefit in improving their farms, and otherwise aiding them in their efforts to become self-supporting. Three schools are in successful operation on their reservation, having in attendance three hundred and twenty-three scholars.

Winnebagoes. — These Indians, numbering one thousand four hundred and forty, a gain of forty over last year, are located in the eastern part of Nebraska, on a reservation containing 128,000 acres, adjoining that of the Omahas, and lying about eighty miles north of the city of Omaha. They are the remnant of a once powerful tribe which formerly inhabited Wisconsin, from which

State they removed to Minnesota under the treaty of 1837. At the outbreak of the Sioux in 1862, they were peaceably engaged in agriculture, in a beautiful and fertile country on the waters of the Blue Earth River, a majority being thriving and industrious farmers, many of them possessing considerable intelligence. Although the Winnebagoes were wholly disconnected with that outbreak, yet the citizens in their immediate vicinity, as well as in other portions of Minnesota, were so determined that all Indians should be removed beyond the limits of the State, that Congress, in 1863, passed an act providing for their removal. They were first removed in May, 1863, to Crow Creek, in Dakota; and after great suffering, and loss of many lives from exposure and starvation, they were finally established upon their present reservation, which had been secured for them by the government under treaty stipulations with the Omahas, and at which they arrived in small and straggling parties during the year 1864. They are now gradually regaining their former comfortable and prosperous condition. Allotments of lands have been made to them. Their agent reports that the past year has been marked by a steady improvement of the condition generally of the tribe. The men have nearly all adopted the dress of the whites; and the agent anticipates that the women will do the same so soon as they shall come to live in houses, a number of which (50), of a better class than is usually provided for Indian occupancy, are now being erected, to be given to those most industrious and making the greatest progress toward civilization. Considerable interest is manifested in education, there being three day-schools, efficiently managed, with an attendance of two hundred and fifty scholars; and there is probably in operation by this date also an industrial and boarding school, capable of accommodating eighty scholars.

Omahas. — The Omahas, a peaceable and inoffensive people, numbering nine hundred and sixty-nine, a decrease since 1871 of fifteen, are native to the country now occupied by them, and occupy a reservation of 345,600 acres adjoining the Winnebagoes. They have lands allotted to them in severalty, and have made considerable advancement in agriculture and civilization, though they still follow the chase to some extent. Under the provisions of the act of June 10, 1872, steps are being taken to sell 50,000 acres of the western part of their reservation. The proceeds of the sale of these lands will enable them to improve and stock their farms, build houses, &c., and, with proper care and industry, to become in a few years entirely self-sustaining. A few cottages are to be found upon this reservation.

There are at present three schools in operation on this reservation, with an attendance of one hundred and twenty scholars.

Pawnees.—The Pawnees, a warlike people, number two thousand four hundred and forty-seven, an increase for the past year of eighty-three. They are located on a reservation of 288,000 acres, in the central part of the State. They are native to the country now occupied by them, and have for years been loyal to the government, having frequently furnished scouts for the army in operations against hostile tribes or marauding bands. Their location, so near the frontier, and almost in constant contact with the Indians of the plains, with whom they have been always more or less at war, has tended to retard their advancement in the arts of civilization. They are, however, gradually becoming more habituated to the customs of the whites, are giving some attention to agriculture, and, with the disappearance of the buffalo from their section of the country, will doubtless settle down to farming and to the practice of mechanical arts in earnest. The act of June 10, 1872, heretofore referred to, provides also for the sale of 50,000 acres belonging to the Pawnees, the same to be taken from that part of their reservation lying south of Loup Fork. These lands are now being surveyed; and it is believed, that, with the proceeds of this sale, such improvements, in the way of building houses and opening and stocking farms, can be made for the Pawnees as will at an early day induce them to give their entire time and attention to industrial pursuits. There are two schools in operation on the reservation, — one a manual-labor boarding-school, the other a day-school, with an attendance at both of one hundred and eighteen scholars. Provision was also made by Congress, at its last session, for the erection of two additional school-houses for the use of this tribe.

Sacs and Foxes of the Missouri. — These Indians, formerly a portion of the same tribe with the Indians now known as the Sacs and Foxes of the Mississippi, emigrated many years ago from Iowa, and settled near the tribe of Iowas, hereafter to be mentioned. They number at the present time but eighty-eight, having been steadily diminishing for years. They have a reservation of about 16,000 acres, lying in the south-eastern part of Nebraska and the north-eastern part of Kansas, purchased for them from the Iowas. Most of it is excellent land; but they have never, to any considerable extent, made use of it for tillage, being almost hopelessly disinclined to engage in labor of any kind, and depending principally for their subsistence, a very poor one, upon their annuity, which is secured to them by the treaty of Oct. 31, 1837, and amounts to $7,870. By act of June 10, 1872, provision was made for the sale of a portion or all of their reservation, the proceeds of such sale to be expended for their immediate use, or for their removal to the Indian Territory or elsewhere. They have consented to the sale of their entire reservation; and, so soon as funds shall have been received from that source, steps will be taken to have them removed to the Indian Territory south of Kansas.

Iowas. — These Indians, numbering at present two hundred and twenty-five, emigrated years ago from Iowa and North-western Missouri, and now have a reservation adjoining the Sacs and Foxes of the Missouri, containing about 16,000 acres. They belong to a much better class of

Indians than their neighbors the Sacs and Foxes, being temperate, frugal, industrious, and interested in the education of their children. They were thoroughly loyal during the late rebellion, and furnished a number of soldiers to the Union army. Many of them are good farmers; and as a tribe they are generally extending their agricultural operations, improving their dwellings, and adding to their comforts. A large majority of the tribe are anxious to have their reservation allotted in severalty; and, inasmuch as they are not inclined to remove to another locality, it would seem desirable that their wishes in this respect should be complied with. One school is in operation on the reservation, with an attendance of sixty-eight scholars, besides an industrial home for orphans, supported by the Indians themselves.

Otoes and Missourias. — These Indians, numbering four hundred and sixty-four, an increase of fourteen over last year, were removed from Iowa and Missouri to their present beautiful and fertile reservation, comprising 160,000 acres, and situated in the southern part of Nebraska. Until quite recently they have evinced but little disposition to labor for a support or in any way to better their miserable condition; yet cut off from their wonted source of subsistence, the buffalo, by their fear of the wild tribes which have taken possession of their old hunting-grounds, they have gradually been more and more forced to work for a living. Within the last three years many of them have opened farms and built themselves houses. A school has also been established, having an attendance of ninety-five scholars.

KANSAS.

The Indians still remaining in Kansas are the Kickapoos, Pottawatomies (Prairie band), Chippewas and Munsees, Miamies, and the Kansas or Kaws.

Kickapoos.—The Kickapoos emigrated from Illinois, and are now located, to the number of two hundred and ninety, on a reservation of 19,200 acres, in the north-eastern part of the State. During the late war a party of about one hundred, dissatisfied with the treaty made with the tribe in 1863, went to Mexico, upon representations made to them by certain of their kinsmen living in that republic, that they would be welcomed and protected by the Mexican government; but, finding themselves deceived, attempted to return to the United States. Only a few, however, succeeded in reaching the Kickapoo agency. The Kickapoos now remaining in Mexico separated from the tribe more than twenty years ago, and settled among the southern Indians in the Indian Territory, on or near the Washita River, whence they went to Mexico, where they still live, notwithstanding the efforts of the government, of late, to arrange with Mexico for their removal to the Indian Territory and location upon some suitable reservation. Their raids across the border have been a sore affliction to the people of Texas; and it is important that the first promising occasion should be taken to secure their return to the United States, and their establishment where they may be carefully watched, and restrained from their depredatory habits, or summarily punished if they persist in them. The Kickapoos remaining in Kansas are peaceable and industrious, continuing to make commendable progress in the cultivation of their farms, and showing much interest in the education of their children. Under the provisions of the treaty of June 28, 1862, a few of these Indians have received lands in severalty, for which patents have been issued, and are now citizens of the United States. Two schools are in operation among these Indians, with a daily average attendance of thirty-nine scholars.

Pottawatomies. — The Prairie band is all of this tribe remaining in Kansas, the rest having become citizens and removed, or most of them, to the Indian Territory. The tribe, excepting those in Wisconsin hererofore noticed, formerly resided in Michigan and Indiana, and removed to Kansas under the provisions of the treaty of 1846. The Prairie band numbers, as nearly as ascertained, about four hundred, and is located on a reserve of 77,357 acres, fourteen miles north of Topeka. Notwithstanding many efforts to educate and civilize these Indians, most of them still cling tenaciously to the habits and customs of their fathers. Some, however, have recently turned their attention to agricultural pursuits, and are now raising stock and most of the varieties of grain produced by their white neighbors. They are also showing more interest in education than formerly; one school being in operation on the reservation, with an attendance of eighty-four scholars.

Chippewas and Munsees. — Certain of the Chippewas of Saginaw, Swan Creek, and Black River, removed from Michigan under the treaty of 1836; and certain Munsees, or Christian Indians, from Wisconsin under the treaty of 1839. These were united by the terms of the treaty concluded with them July 16, 1859. The united bands now number only fifty-six. They own 4,760 acres of land in Franklin County, about forty miles south of the town of Lawrence, holding the same in severalty, are considerably advanced in the arts of life, and earn a decent living, principally by agriculture. They have one school in operation, with an attendance of sixteen scholars. These Indians, at present, have no treaty with the United States; nor do they receive any assistance from the government.

Miamies.—The Miamies of Kansas formerly resided in Indiana, forming one tribe with the Miamies still remaining in that State, but removed in 1846 to their present location, under the provisions of the treaty of 1840.

Owing to the secession of a considerable number who have allied themselves with the Peorias, in the Indian Territory, and also to the ravages of disease consequent on vicious indulgences, especially in the use of intoxicating drinks, this band, which, on its removal from Indiana, embraced about five hundred, at present numbers but ninety-five. These have a reservation of 10,240 acres in Linn and Miami Counties, in the south-east part of Kansas, the larger part of which is held in severalty by them.

The Superintendent of Indian Affairs, in immediate charge, in his report for this year says the Miamies remaining in Kansas are greatly demoralized, their school has been abandoned, and their youth left destitute of educational advantages.

Considerable trouble has been for years caused by white settlers locating aggressively on lands belonging to these Indians, no effort for their extrusion having been thus far successful.

Kansas or Kaws. — These Indians are native to the country they occupy. They number at present five hundred and ninety-three: in 1860 they numbered eight hundred and three. Although they have a reservation of 80,640 acres of good land in the eastern part of the State, they are poor and improvident, and have in late years suffered much for want of the actual necessaries of life. They never were much disposed to labor, depending upon the chase for a living, in connection with the annuities due from government.

They have been growing steadily poorer; and even now, in their straitened circumstances, and under the pressure of want, they show but little inclination to engage in agricultural pursuits, all attempts to induce them to work having measurably proved failures. Until quite recently they could not even be prevailed upon to have their children educated. One school is now in operation, with an attendance of about forty-five scholars. By the act of May 8, 1872, provision was made for the sale of all the lands owned by these Indians in Kansas, and for their removal to the Indian Territory. Provision was also made, by the act of June 5, 1872, for their settlement within the limits of a tract of land therein provided to be set apart for the Osages. Their lands in Kansas are now being appraised by commissioners appointed for the purpose, preparatory to their sale.

INDIAN TERRITORY.

The Indians at present located in the Indian Territory — an extensive district, bounded north by Kansas, east by Missouri and Arkansas, south by Texas, and west by the one hundredth meridian, designated by the commissioners appointed under act of Congress July 20, 1867, to establish peace with certain hostile tribes, as one of two great Territories (the other being, in the main, the present Territory of Dakota, west of the Missouri) upon which might be concentrated the great body of all the Indians east of the Rocky Mountains — are the Cherokees, Choctaws, Chickasaws, Creeks, Seminoles, Senecas, Shawnees, Quapaws, Ottawas of Blanchard's Fork and Roche de Bœuf, Peorias, and confederated Kaskaskias, Weas and Piankeshaws, Wyandots, Pottawatomies, Sacs and Foxes of the Mississippi, Osages, Kiowas, Comanches, the Arapahoes and Cheyennes of the south, the Wichitas and other affiliated bands, and a small band of Apaches long confederated with the Kiowas and Comanches.

Cherokees. — The Cherokees number, according to the census for 1872, furnished by their agent, 18,000. In the report for 1871 the agent estimated the number at 14,682, and stated that if the Cherokees remaining in North Carolina and other States were gathered into the nation, the population would then be 16,500. He does not now account for the large increase over the enumeration for 1871, which must be due to a gross error in one report or the other. The Cherokees occupy a reservation of 3,844,712 acres in the north-eastern part of the Territory, lying east of the 96° west longitude. They also own a strip about fifty miles wide adjoining Kansas on the south, and extending from the Arkansas River west to the 100° west longitude. By the treaty of 1866, however, the United States may settle friendly Indians within the limits of the latter tract; and when such settlements are made the rights of the Cherokees to the lands so occupied terminate, the lands thus disposed of to be paid for to the Cherokee nation at such price as may be agreed upon by the parties in interest, or as may be fixed by the President. That portion of country lying between the 96° west longitude on the east, the Arkansas River on the west and south, and the State of Kansas on the north, formerly owned by the Cherokees, has been sold to the Osages.

The Cherokees originally inhabited sections of country now embraced within the State of Georgia and portions of the States of Tennessee and North Carolina, and moved to their present location under the provisions of the treaties concluded with them in 1817 and 1835. They have their own written language, their national constitution and laws, their churches, schools, and academies, their judges and courts. They are emphatically an agricultural and stock-raising people, and perhaps of all the Indian tribes, great and small, are first in general intelligence, in the acquisition of wealth, in the knowledge of the useful arts, and in social and moral progress. The evidences of a real and substantial advancement in these respects are too clear to be questioned; and it is the more remarkable from the fact, that, but a few years since, they were, as a people, almost ruined by the ravages of civil war. Their dwellings consist of 500 frame-houses, and 3,500 log-houses. Of the principal crops, they have raised during the year 2,925,000 bushels of corn, 97,500 bushels of wheat, about the same quantity of oats, and 80,000 bushels of potatoes. Their stock consists of 16,000 horses, 75,000 cattle, 160,000 hogs, and 9,000 sheep. The individual wealth is estimated at $4,995,000.

By the latest reports, they had sixty schools in successful operation, all, with the exception of one managed by the Moravians, maintained out of the national school-fund, and having in attendance 2,133 scholars. Three of these schools are for the education of the freedmen living in the country. The orphans of the Cherokees have been heretofore provided for in private families, by means of the interest derived from certain funds invested for that purpose; but during the past year an orphan asylum has been established under an act of the National Council, where are now gathered fifty-four of this class. This school is designed ultimately to embrace in its operations all the orphans of the nation.

The Cherokees have no treaty-funds paid to them or expended for their benefit. They have, however, United-States and State bonds held in trust for them by the Secretary of the Interior, to the amount of $1,633,627.39; also a recognized claim on account of abstracted State bonds to the amount of $83,000, on which the interest is appropriated annually by Congress, making in all $1,716,627.39. This sum is divided under the following heads, viz., national fund, $1,008,285.07; school fund, $532,407.01; orphan fund, $175,935.31. The interest on these several sums is paid to the treasurer of the Cherokee nation, to be used under the direction of the National Council for the objects indicated by said heads.

Choctaws and Chickasaws. — These tribes are for certain national purposes confederated. The Choctaws, numbering 16,000, an increase of 1,000 on the enumeration for 1871, have a reservation of

6,688,000 acres in the south-eastern part of the Territory; and the Chickasaws, numbering 6,000, own a tract containing 4,377,600 acres adjoining the Choctaws on the west. These tribes originally inhabited the section of country now embraced within the State of Mississippi, and were removed to their present location in accordance with the terms of the treaties concluded with them, respectively, in 1820 and 1832. The remarks made respecting the language, laws, educational advantages, industrial pursuits, and advancement in the arts and customs of civilized life, of the Cherokees, will apply in the main to the Choctaws and Chickasaws. The Choctaws have 36 schools in operation, with an attendance of 819 scholars; the Chickasaws 11, with 379 scholars. The Choctaws, under the treaties of Nov. 16, 1805, Oct. 18, 1820, Jan. 20, 1825, and June 22, 1855, receive permanent annuities as follows: in money, $3,000; for support of government, education, and other beneficial purposes, $25,512.89; for support of light-horsemen, $600; and for iron and steel, $320. They also have United-States and State stocks, held in trust for them by the Secretary of the Interior, to the amount of $506,427.20, divided as follows: on account of "Choctaw general fund,"

$454,000; of "Choctaw school-fund," $52,427.20. The interest on these funds, and the annuities, &c., are turned over to the treasurer of the nation, and expended under the direction of the National Council in the manner and for the objects indicated in each case. The Chickasaws, under act of Feb. 25, 1799, and treaty of April 28, 1866, have a permanent annuity of $3,000. They also have United-States and State stocks, held in trust for them by the Secretary of the Interior, to the amount of $1,185,947.03⅔; $183,947.03⅔ thereof being a "national fund," and $2,000 a fund for "incompetents." The interest on these sums, and the item of $3,000 first referred to, are paid over to the treasurer of the nation, and disbursed by him, under the direction of the National Council, and for such objects as that body may determine.

Creeks. — The Creeks came originally from Alabama and Georgia. They numbered at the latest date of enumeration 12,295, and have a reservation of 3,215,495 acres in the eastern and central part of the Territory. They are not generally so far advanced as the Cherokees, Choctaws, and Chickasaws, but are making rapid progress, and will doubtless, in a few years, rank in all respects with their neighbors, the three tribes just named.

The Creeks, by the latest reports, have 33 schools in operation; one of which is under the management of the Methodist Mission Society, and another supported by the Presbyterians. The number of scholars in all the schools is 760. These Indians have, under treaties of Aug. 7, 1790, June 16, 1802, Jan. 24, 1826, Aug. 7, 1856, and June 14, 1866, permanent annuities and interest on moneys uninvested as follows: in money, $68,258.40; for pay of blacksmiths and assistants, wagon-maker, wheelwright, iron and steel, $3,250; for assistance in agricultural operations, $2,000; and for education, $1,000. The Secretary of the Interior holds in trust for certain members of the tribe, known as "orphans," United-States and State bonds to the amount of $76,999.66, the interest on which sum is paid to those of said orphans who are alive, and to the representatives of those who have deceased.

Seminoles. — The Seminoles, numbering 2,398, an increase of 190 over the census of 1871, have a reservation of 200,000 acres adjoining the Creeks on the west. This tribe formerly inhabited the section of country now embraced in the State of Florida. Some of them removed to their present location under the provisions of the treaties of

1832 and 1833. The remainder of the tribe, instigated by the former chief, Osceola, repudiated the treaties, refused to remove, and soon after commenced depredating upon the whites. In 1835 these depredations resulted in war, which continued seven years, with immense cost of blood and treasure. The Indians were at last rendered powerless to do further injury, and, after efforts repeated through several years, were finally, with the exception of a few who fled to the everglades, removed to a reservation in the now Indian Territory. In 1866 they ceded to the United States, by treaty, the reservation then owned by them, and purchased the tract they at present occupy. They are not so far advanced in the arts of civilized life as the Cherokees, Choctaws, Chickasaws, and Creeks, but are making rapid progress in that direction, and will, it is confidently believed, soon rank with the tribes named. They cultivate 7,600 acres; upon which they raised during the past year 300,000 bushels of corn, and 6,000 bushels of potatoes. They live in log-houses, and own large stocks of cattle, horses, and hogs. The schools of the Seminoles number 4, with an attendance of 169 scholars.

They receive, under treaties made with them

Aug. 7, 1856, and March 21, 1866, annuities, &c., as follows: interest on $500,000, amounting to $25,000 annually, which is paid to them as annuity; interest on $50,000, amounting to $2,500 annually, for support of schools; and $1,000, the interest on $20,000, for the support of their government.

Senecas and Shawnees. — The Senecas, numbering 214, and the Shawnees, numbering 90, at the present time, removed, some thirty-five or forty years ago, from Ohio to their present location in the north-eastern corner of the Territory. They suffered severely during the rebellion, being obliged to leave their homes and fly to the North, their country being devastated by troops of both armies. Under the provisions of the treaty of 1867, made with these and other tribes, the Senecas, who were then confederated with the Shawnees, dissolved their connection with that tribe, sold to the United States their half of the reservation owned by them in common with the Shawnees, and connected themselves with those Senecas who then owned a separate reservation. The Shawnees now have a reservation of 24,960 acres, and the united Senecas one of 44,000 acres. These tribes are engaged in agriculture to a considerable extent. They are peaceable and industrious. Many are thrifty farmers, and in comfortable circumstances. They have one school in operation, with an attendance of 36 scholars, which includes some children of the Wyandots, which tribe has no schools.

Quapaws. — These Indians number at the present time about 240. They are native to the country, and occupy a reservation of 104,000 acres in the extreme north-east corner of the Territory. They do not appear to have advanced much within the past few years. In common with other tribes in that section, they suffered greatly by the late war, and were rendered very destitute. Their proximity to the border towns of Kansas, and the facilities thereby afforded for obtaining whiskey, have tended to retard their progress; but there has recently been manifested a strong desire for improvement; and with the funds derived from the sale of a part of their lands, and with the proposed opening of a school among them, better things are hoped for in the future.

Ottawas. — The Ottawas of Blanchard's Fork and Roche de Bœuf number, at the present time, 150. They were originally located in Western Ohio and Southern Michigan, and were removed, in accordance with the terms of the treaty concluded with them in 1831, to a reservation within the present limits of Kansas. Under the treaty of 1867 they obtained a reservation of 24,960 acres, lying immediately north of the western portion of the Shawnee reservation. They have paid considerable attention to education, are well advanced in civilization, and many of them are industrious and prosperous farmers. They have one school, attended by 52 scholars. The relation of this small band to the government is somewhat anomalous, inasmuch as, agreeably to provisions contained in the treaties of 1862 and 1867, they have become citizens of the United States, and yet reside in the Indian Country, possess a reservation there, and maintain a purely tribal organization. They removed from Franklin Co., Kan., in 1870.

Peorias, &c.—The Peorias, Kaskaskias, Weas, and Piankeshaws, who were confederated in 1854, and at that time had a total population of 259, now number 160. They occupy a reservation of 72,000 acres, adjoining the Quapaw reservation on the south and west. Under treaties made with these tribes in 1832, they removed to a tract within the present limits of Kansas, where they remained until after the treaty of 1867 was concluded with them, in which treaty provision was made whereby they obtained their present reservation. These Indians are generally intelligent, well advanced in civilization, and, to judge from the statistical reports of their agent, are very successful in their agricultural operations, raising crops ample for their own support. With the Peorias are about 40 Miamies from Kansas. They have one school in operation, with an attendance of 29 scholars.

Wyandots. — The Wyandots number at the present time 222 souls. Ten years ago there were 435. They occupy a reservation of 20,000 acres, lying between the Seneca and Shawnee reservations. This tribe was located for many years in North-western Ohio, whence they removed, pursuant to the terms of the treaty made with them in 1842, to a reservation within the present limits of Kansas. By the treaty made with them in 1867, their present reservation was set apart for those members of the tribe who desired to maintain their tribal organization, instead of becoming citizens, as provided in the treaty of 1855. They are poor, and, having no annuities and but little force of character, are making slight progress in industry or civilization. They have been lately joined by members of the tribe, who, under the treaty, accepted citizenship. These, desiring to resume their relations with their people, have been again adopted into the tribe.

Pottawatomies. — These Indians, who formerly resided in Michigan and Indiana, whence they removed to Kansas, before going down into the Indian Territory numbered about 1,600. They have, under the provisions of the treaty of 1861 made with the tribe, then residing in Kansas, become citizens of the United States. By the terms of said treaty they received allotments of land, and their proportion of the tribal funds, with the exception of their share of certain non-paying State stocks, amounting to sixty-seven thousand dollars, held in trust by the Secretary of the Interior for the Pottawatomies. Having disposed of their lands, they removed to the Indian Territory, where a reservation thirty miles square, adjoining the Seminole reservation on the west, had been, by the treaty of 1867, provided for such as should elect to maintain their tribal organization. It having been decided, however, by the department, that, as they had all become citizens, there was consequently no part of the tribe remaining which could lay claim, under treaty stipulations, to the reservation in the Indian Territory, legislation was had by Congress at its last session — act approved May 23, 1872 — by which these citizen Pottawatomies were allowed allotments of land within the tract originally assigned for their use as a tribe, to the extent of one hundred and sixty acres to each head of family and to each other person twenty-one years of age, and of eighty acres to each minor. Most if not all of them are capable of taking care of themselves; and many of them are well-educated, intelligent, and thrifty farmers.

Absentee Shawnees. — These Indians, numbering six hundred and sixty-three, separated about thirty years ago from the main tribe, then located in Kansas, and settled in the Indian Territory, principally within the limits of the thirty miles square tract heretofore referred to in the remarks relative to the Pottawatomies, where they engaged in farming, and have since supported themselves without assistance from the government.

Sacs and Foxes. — The Sacs and Foxes of the Mississippi number at the present time 463. In 1846 they numbered 2,478. They have a reservation of 483,840 acres, adjoining the Creeks on the west, and between the North Fork of the

Canadian and the Red Fork of the Arkansas Rivers. They formerly occupied large tracts of country in Wisconsin, Iowa, and Missouri, whence they removed, by virtue of treaty stipulations, to a reservation within the present limits of Kansas. By the terms of the treaties of 1859 and 1868, all their lands in Kansas were ceded to the United States, and they were given in lieu thereof their present reservation. These Indians, once famous for their prowess in war, have not, for some years, made any marked improvement upon their former condition. Still they have accomplished a little, under highly adverse circumstances and influences, in the way of opening small farms and in building houses, and are beginning to show some regard for their women by relieving them of the burdens and labors heretofore required of them. There is hope of their further improvement, although they are still but one degree removed from the Blanket or Breech-Clout Indians. They have one school in operation, with an attendance of only about twelve scholars. 317 members of these tribes, after their removal to Kansas, returned to Iowa, where they were permitted to remain, and are now, under the act of March 2, 1867, receiving their share of the tribal funds. They have purchased 419 acres of land in Tama County, part of which they are cultivating. They are not much disposed to work, however, on lands of their own, preferring to labor for the white farmers in their vicinity, and are still much given to roving and hunting.

Osages. — The Osages, numbering 3,956, are native to the general section of country where they now live. Their reservation is bounded on the north by the south line of Kansas, east by the ninety-sixth degree of west longitude, and south and west by the Arkansas River, and contains approximately 1,760,000 acres. They still follow the chase, the buffalo being their main dependence for food. Their wealth consists in horses (of which they own not less than 12,000) and in cattle.

Kiowas, Comanches, and Apaches. — These tribes, confederated under present treaty stipulations, formerly ranged over an extensive country lying between the Rio Grande and the Red River. As nearly as can be ascertained, they number as follows: Kiowas, 1,930; Comanches, 3,180; and Apaches, 380. They are now located upon a reservation secured to them by treaty made in

1867, comprising 3,549,440 acres in the south-western part of the Indian Territory, west of and adjoining the Chickasaw country. Wild and intractable, these Indians, even the best of them, have given small signs of improvement in the arts of life ; and, substantially, the whole dealing of the government with them, thus far, has been in the way of supplying their necessities for food and clothing, with a view to keeping them upon their reservation, and preventing their raiding into Texas, with the citizens of which State they were for many years before their present establishment on terms of mutual hatred and injury. Some individuals and bands have remained quiet and peaceable upon their reservation, evincing a disposition to learn the arts of life, to engage in agriculture, and to have their children instructed in letters. To these every inducement is being held out to take up land, and actively commence tilling it. Thus far they have under cultivation but 100 acres, which have produced the past year a good crop of corn and potatoes. The wealth of these tribes consists in horses and mules, of which they own to the number, as reported by their agent, of 16,500, a great proportion of the animals notoriously having been stolen in Texas.

However, it may be said, in a word, of these Indians, that their civilization must follow their submission to the government, and that the first necessity in respect to them is a wholesome example, which shall inspire fear and command obedience. So long as four-fifths of these tribes take turns at raiding into Texas, openly and boastfully bringing back scalps and spoils to their reservation, efforts to inspire very high ideas of social and industrial life among the communities of which the raiders form so large a part will presumably result in failure.

Arapahoes and Cheyennes of the South. — These tribes are native to the section of country now inhabited by them. The Arapahoes number at the present time 1,500, and the Cheyennes 2,000. By the treaty of 1867, made with these Indians, a large reservation was provided for them, bounded on the north by Kansas, on the east by the Arkansas River, and on the south and west by the Red Fork of the Arkansas. They have, however, persisted in a refusal to locate on this reservation; and another tract, containing 4,011,500 acres, north of and adjoining the Kiowa and Comanche reservation, was set apart for them by Executive order of Aug. 10, 1869. By act of May 29,

1872, the Secretary of the Interior was authorized to negotiate with these Indians for the relinquishment of their claim to the lands ceded to them by the said treaty, and to give them in lieu thereof a "sufficient and permanent location" upon lands ceded to the United States by the Creeks and Seminoles in treaties made with them in 1866. Negotiations to the end proposed were duly entered into with these tribes unitedly; but, in the course of such negotiations, it has become the view of this Office that the tribes should no longer be associated in the occupation of a reservation. The Arapahoes are manifesting an increasing disinclination to follow further the fortunes of the Cheyennes, and crave a location of their own. Inasmuch as the conduct of the Arapahoes is uniformly good, and their disposition to make industrial improvement very decided, it is thought that they should now be separated from the more turbulent Cheyennes, and given a place where they may carry out their better intentions without interruption and without the access of influences tending to draw their young men away to folly and mischief. With this view a contract, made subject to the action of Congress, was entered into between the Commissioner of

Indian Affairs and the delegation of the Arapaho tribe which visited Washington during the present season (the delegation being fully empowered thereto by the tribe), by which the Arapahoes relinquish all their interest in the reservation granted them by the treaty of 1867, in consideration of the grant of a reservation between the North Fork of the Canadian River and the Red Fork of the Arkansas River, and extending from a point ten miles east of the ninety-eighth to near the ninety-ninth meridian of west longitude. Should this adjustment of the question, so far as the Arapahoes are concerned, meet the approval of Congress, separate negotiations will be entered into with the Cheyennes, with a view to obtaining their relinquishment of the reservation of 1867, and their location on some vacant tract within the same general section of the Indian Territory.

A considerable number of the Arapahoes are already engaged in agriculture, though at a disadvantage; and, when the question of their reservation shall have been settled, it is confidently believed that substantially the whole body of this tribe will turn their attention to the cultivation of the soil. Two schools are conducted for their benefit at the agency, having an attendance of thirty-five scholars. Of the Cheyennes confederated with the Arapahoes, the reports are less favorable as to progress made in industry, or disposition to improve their condition. Until 1867 both these tribes, in common with the Kiowas and Comanches, were engaged in hostilities against the white settlers in Western Kansas; but since the treaty made with them in that year they have, with the exception of one small band of the Cheyennes, remained friendly, and have committed no depredations.

Wichitas, &c. — The Wichitas and other affiliated bands of Keechies, Wacoes, Towoccaroes, Caddoes, Ionies, and Delawares, number 1,250, divided approximately as follows: Wichitas, 299; Keechies, 126; Wacoes, 140; Towoccaroes, 127; Caddoes, 392; Ionies, 85; Delawares, 81. These Indians, fragments of once important tribes originally belonging in Louisiana, Texas, Kansas, and the Indian Territory, were all, excepting the Wichitas and Delawares, removed by the government from Texas, in 1859, to the "leased district," then belonging to the Choctaws and Chickasaws, where they have since resided, at a point on the Washita River near old Fort Cobb. They have no treaty relations with the government; nor have they any defined reservation. They have always, or at least for many years, been friendly to the whites, although in close and constant contact with the Kiowas and Comanches. A few of them, chiefly Caddoes and Delawares, are engaged in agriculture, and are disposed to be industrious. Of the other Indians at this agency, some cultivate small patches in corn and vegetables, the work being done mainly by women; but the most are content to live upon the government. The Caddoes rank among the best Indians of the continent, and set an example to the other bands affiliated with them worthy of being more generally followed than it is. In physique, and in the virtues of chastity, temperance, and industry, they are the equals of many white communities.

A permanent reservation should be set aside for the Indians of this agency; and, with proper assistance, they would doubtless in a few years become entirely self-sustaining. But one school is in operation, with an attendance of eighteen scholars. These Indians have no annuities; but an annual appropriation of $50,000 has for several years been made for their benefit. This money is expended for goods and agricultural implements, and for assistance and instruction in farming, &c.

DAKOTA, MONTANA, WYOMING, AND IDAHO.

The tribes residing in Dakota, Montana, Wyoming, and Idaho are divided as follows: in Dakota, about 28,000; Montana, 30,000; Wyoming, 2,000; and Idaho, 5,000. The present temporary location of the Red Cloud agency has, however, drawn just within the limits of Wyoming a body of Indians varying from 8,000 to 9,000, who are here, and usually, reckoned as belonging in Dakota.

DAKOTA.

The Indians within the limits of Dakota Territory are the Sioux, the Poncas, and the Arickarees, Gros Ventres, and Mandans.

Sioux. — There are probably, including those at the Red Cloud agency, at present temporarily located in Wyoming, about 25,000 Sioux under the care of government at eight different agencies.

The Yankton Sioux, numbering about 2,000, are located in the extreme southern part of the Territory, on the east side of the Missouri, about fifty miles from the town of Yankton, upon a reservation of 400,000 acres, nearly all rolling prairie, set apart for them by treaty of 1858, out of the tract then ceded by them to the United States. They have not been much inclined to work; and, although there is good land within their reservation, they are poor, having still to be subsisted in a great measure by the government. It is but due to say of the Yanktons, that, while other bands of Sioux have been hostile to the government and citizens, they have uniformly been friendly, even to the extent of assisting the government against their own kindred. They are now giving considerable attention to the education of their children, having six schools in operation, with an average attendance of three hundred and sixty-six scholars.

The Sisseton and Wahpeton bands have two reservations, — one in the eastern part of the Territory, at Lake Traverse, containing 1,241,600 acres, where are 1,496 Indians; and one in the north-eastern part of the Territory, at Devil's Lake, containing 345,600 acres, where are 720 Indians, including a few from the "Cut-Head" band of Sioux. These two reservations are provided for in a treaty made with the bands in 1867. These Indians were a portion of the Sioux living in Minnesota at the time of the outbreak in 1862. Many of them claim to have been, and doubtless were, friendly to the whites during the troubles referred to; and when the removal of the Sioux took place in 1863, as noticed heretofore under the title of "Santee Sioux," they went to the western part of Minnesota and to the eastern and northern parts of Dakota, near their present reservations. They are quite generally engaged in agricultural operations, under the system adopted while they were on their reservation in Minnesota, by which the individual Indians receive pay in goods or supplies for all work performed, only the aged, infirm, or sick being supplied with clothing and subsistence gratuitously. So far as these Indians are concerned, the scheme has been decidedly successful; and it should be extended to all the tribes and bands now on the "feeding-list," so soon as practicable. There are four schools in operation for the bands at Lake Traverse, attended by one hundred and twenty-three scholars. An unusual degree of interest is manifested of late in having their children educated. By treaty made with them in 1867, the amount of funds to be appropriated annually for their benefit is at the discretion of Congress. For the present year, the sum of $75,000 has been appropriated for the benefit of these Indians. They also participate in the proceeds derived from the sales of the Sioux lands in Minnesota, which furnish a considerable revenue yearly.

The Oncpapa, Blackfeet, Lower Yanktonai, Upper Yanktonai, Sans Arc, Upper and Lower Brulé, Two Kettle, Minneconjou, and Ogallala bands are located at five different agencies, viz.: the Upper Missouri, or Crow Creek agency, on the east side of the Missouri; the Grand River agency, at the mouth of the Grand River; the Cheyenne River agency, at the mouth of the Cheyenne River; the Whetstone agency (so called from its former location at the junction of the Whetstone with the Missouri Rivers), on the White River, about two hundred and twenty-five miles west of the Missouri; and the Red Cloud agency, at present on the North Platte, about thirty miles south-east from Fort Laramie. The Indians at these agencies number in the aggregate about 22,000. They have a reservation set apart for them by the treaty of 1868, containing about 25,000,000 acres, lying west of the Missouri River and north of Nebraska. Prior to this treaty, these Indians had for years been engaged in acts of hostility against the government and in depredations upon the white settlers. Claiming to own most, if not all, of the Territory of Dakota, and portions of the Territories of Montana and Wyoming, as well as the western part of Nebraska, they used every effort to prevent the settlement of the country so claimed, their hostility being especially directed against the Union Pacific Railroad. The military operations of 1867–68, however, convinced the Sioux of the hopelessness of opposing the progress of the railroad, and the settlement of the immediate belt through which it was to pass, and disposed them to accept the provision made for them by the treaty of 1868. With the exception of the main portion of the Ogallala band, at the Red Cloud agency, and a considerable body of disaffected Indians from all the bands, known as the "hostile Sioux," of whom "Sitting Bull" and "Black Moon" are the principal chiefs, these bands are all within the limits of the reservation set apart by said treaty of 1868. A few at each of the agencies on the Missouri River have shown a disposition to engage in agriculture; but by far the greater part of them remain "breech-clout" Indians, disinclined to labor for a living, and accepting subsistence from the government as the natural and proper consideration for the favor done the government by their consenting to remain at the agencies assigned them. If they have any suspicion that this thing cannot last forever, and that the time will soon come for them to work or starve, the great majority do not allow themselves to be influenced by it, but seem determined to put the evil day as far off as possible.

Poncas. — The Poncas, numbering 735, have a reservation of 576,000 acres, near the confluence of the Niobrara and Missouri Rivers, in the south-eastern part of the Territory, provided for them in their treaty with the United States, made in 1858. They are quiet and peaceable, are inclined to be industrious, and engage to some extent in farming; but from various causes, principally the destruction of their crops by grasshoppers, have not succeeded in supporting themselves without assistance from the government. They are well advanced in civilized habits of life, and have shown considerable interest in the education of their children, having three schools in operation, with an average attendance of seventy-seven scholars.

Arickarees, Gros Ventres, and Mandans. — These tribes number 2,200, and have a reservation set apart for their occupancy by executive order of April 12, 1870, comprising 8,640,000 acres, situated in the north-western part of Dakota and the eastern part of Montana, extending to the Yellowstone and Powder Rivers. They have no treaty with the government, are now and have always been friendly to the whites, are exceptionally known to the officers of the army and to frontiersmen as "good Indians," and are engaged to some extent in agriculture. Owing to the shortness of the agricultural season, the rigor of the climate, and the periodical ravages of grasshoppers, their efforts in this direction, though made with a degree of patience and perseverance not usual in the Indian character, have met with frequent and distressing reverses; and it has from time to time been found necessary to furnish them with more or less subsistence to prevent starvation. They are traditional enemies of the Sioux; and the petty warfare maintained between them and the Sioux of the Grand River and Cheyenne River agencies — while, like most warfare confined to Indians alone, it causes wonderfully little loss of life — serves to disturb the condition of these agencies, and to retard the progress of all the parties concerned. These Indians should be moved to the Indian

Territory, south of Kansas, where the mildness of the climate and the fertility of the soil would repay their labors, and where, it is thought, from their willingness to labor and their docility under the control of the government, they would in a few years become wholly self-supporting. The question of their removal has been submitted to them; and they seem inclined to favor the project, but have expressed a desire to send a delegation of their chiefs to the Indian Territory, with a view of satisfying themselves as to the desirableness of the location. Their wishes in this respect should be granted early next season, that their removal and settlement may be effected during the coming year. Notwithstanding their willingness to labor, they have shown but little interest in education. Congress makes an appropriation of $75,000 annually for goods and provisions, for their instruction in agricultural and mechanical pursuits, for salaries of employés, and for the education of their children, &c.

MONTANA.

The Indian tribes residing within the limits of Montana are the Blackfeet, Bloods, and Piegans, the Gros Ventres of the Prairie, the Assinaboines, the Yanktonais, Santee and Teton (so called) Sioux, a portion of the northern Arapahoes and Cheyennes, the River Crows, the Mountain Crows, the Flatheads, Pend d'Oreilles, and Kootenays, and a few Shoshones, Bannocks, and Sheep-Eaters, numbering in the aggregate about 32,412. They are all, or nearly all, native to the regions now occupied by them respectively.

The following table will exhibit the population of each of these tribes, as nearly as the same can be ascertained: —

Tribe	Population
Blackfeet, Bloods, and Piegans	7,500
Assinaboines	4,790
Gros Ventres	1,100
Santee, Yanktonais, Uncpapa, and Cut-Head Sioux, at Milk River agency	2,625
River Crows	1,240
Mountain Crows	2,700
Flatheads	460
Pend d'Oreilles	1,000
Kootenays	320
Shoshones, Bannocks, and Sheep-Eaters	677
Roving Sioux, commonly called Teton Sioux, including those gathered during 1872, at and near Fort Peck, (largely estimated)	8,000
Estimated total	30,412

The number of northern Cheyennes and Arapahoes roaming in Montana, who, it is believed, have co-operated with the Sioux under "Sitting Bull," in their depredations, is not known: it is probably less than 1,000.

The Blackfeet, Bloods, and Piegans (located at the Blackfeet agency on the Teton River, about seventy-five miles from Fort Benton), the Gros Ventres, Assinaboines, the River Crows, about 1,000 of the Northern Arapahoes and Cheyennes, and the Santee and Yankton Sioux (located at the Milk River agency, on the Milk River, about one hundred miles from its mouth), occupy jointly a reservation in the extreme northern part of the Territory, set apart by treaties (not ratified) made in 1868 with most of the tribes named, and containing about 17,408,000 acres. The Blackfeet, Bloods, and Piegans, particularly the last-named band, have been, until within about two years, engaged in depredating upon the white settlers. The Indians at the Milk River agency, with the exception of the Sioux, are now, and have been for several years, quiet and peaceable. The Sioux at this agency, or most of them, were engaged in the outbreak in Minnesota in 1862. On the suppression of hostilities they fled to the northern part of Dakota, where they continued roaming until, in the fall of 1871, they went to their present location, with the avowed intention of remaining there. Although they had been at war for years with the Indians properly belonging to the Milk River agency, yet, by judicious management on the part of the agent of the government stationed there, and the influence of some of the most powerful chiefs, the former feuds and difficulties were amicably arranged; and all parties have remained friendly to each other during the year past. The Indians at neither the Blackfeet nor the Milk River agency show any disposition to engage in farming; nor have they thus far manifested any desire for the education of their children. They rely entirely upon the chase and upon the bounty of the government for their support. They, however, quite scrupulously respect their obligation to preserve the peace; and no considerable difficulty has of late been experienced, or is anticipated, in keeping them in order. The Blackfeet, Bloods, and Piegans have an annual appropriation of $50,000 made for their benefit; the Assinaboines, $30,000; the Gros Ventres of the Prairie, $35,000; the River Crows, $30,000. These funds are used in furnishing the respective tribes with goods and subsistence, and generally for such other objects as may be deemed necessary to keep the Indians quiet.

Mountain Crows. — These Indians have a reservation of 6,272,000 acres, lying in the southern part of the Territory, between the Yellowstone River and the north line of Wyoming Territory. They have always been friendly to the whites, but are inveterate enemies of the Sioux, with whom they have for years been at war. By the treaty of 1868 — by the terms of which their present reservation was set apart for their occupancy — they are liberally supplied with goods, clothing, and subsistence. But few of them are engaged in farming, the main body relying upon their success in hunting, and upon the supplies furnished by the government, for their support. They have one school in operation, with an attendance, however, of only nine scholars. By the treaty of May 7, 1868, provision is made by which they are to receive for a limited number of years the following annuities, &c., viz.: in clothing and goods, $22,723 (twenty-six instalments due); in beneficial objects, $25,000 (six instalments due); in subsistence, $131,400 (one instalment due). Blacksmiths, teachers, physician, carpenter, miller, engineer, and farmer are also furnished for their benefit, at an expense to the government of $11,600.

Flatheads, &c.—The Flatheads, Pend d'Oreilles, and Kootenays have a reservation of 1,433,600 acres in the Jocko Valley, situated in the north-western part of the Territory, and secured to them by treaty of 1855. This treaty also provided for a reservation in the Bitter-Root Valley, should the President of the United States deem it advisable to set apart another for their use. The Flat-heads have remained in the last-named valley; but under the provisions of the act of June 5, 1872, steps are being taken for their removal to the Jocko reservation. Many of these Indians are engaged in agriculture; but, as they receive little assistance from the government, their progress in this direction is slow. They have one school in operation, with an attendance of 27 scholars.

Shoshones, &c.—The Shoshones, Bannocks, and Sheep-Eaters are at present located about twenty miles above the mouth of the Lemhi Fork of the Salmon River, near the western boundary of the Territory. They have shown considerable interest in agriculture; and many of them are quite successful as farmers. They have no reservation set apart for them, either by treaty or by executive order. They are so few in number that it would probably be better to remove them, with their consent, to the Fort Hall reservation in Idaho, where their brethren are located, than to provide them with a separate reservation. They have no schools in operation. An annual appropriation of $25,000 is made for these Indians, which sum is expended for their benefit in the purchase of clothing, subsistence, agricultural implements, &c.

WYOMING.

The Indians in this Territory, with the exception of the Sioux and Northern Arapahoes and Cheyennes, mentioned under the heads of Dakota and Montana respectively, are the eastern band of Shoshones, numbering about 1,000. The Shoshones are native to the country. Their reservation in the Wind River Valley, containing 2,688,000 acres, was set apart for them by treaty of 1868.

But little advancement in civilization has been made by these Indians, owing to their indisposition to labor for a living, and to the incessant incursions into their country of the Sioux and the Northern Arapahoes and Cheyennes, with which tribes they have for many years been at war. The losses sustained from these incursions, and the dread which they inspire, tend to make the Shoshones unsettled, and unwilling to remain continuously on the reservation. They therefore spend most of the year in roaming and hunting when they should be at work tilling the soil and improving their lands. There is one school at the agency, having an attendance of ten scholars, in charge of an Episcopal missionary as teacher.

IDAHO.

The Indian tribes in Idaho are the Nez Percés, the Boisé and Bruneau Shoshones, and Bannocks, the Cœur d'Alênes, and Spokanes, with several other small bands, numbering in the aggregate about 5,800 souls.

Nez Percés. — The Nez Percés number 2,807, and have a reservation of 1,344,000 acres in the northern part of the Territory. By treaties of 1855 and 1863, they ceded to the United States a large body of land lying within the limits of the then Territories of Oregon and Washington, and accepted their present diminished reservation, with certain annuities in consideration of the cession of the remainder. The tribe has long been divided into factions known as the "treaty" party and the "non-treaty" party, from disagreements arising out of the treaty made with them in 1863. Though the ill feeling engendered has in a measure subsided, the "non-treaty" Indians, to the number of a few hundred, still stand apart and accept no favors from the government. These, with few exceptions, reside outside the reservation, on Snake River and its tributaries, and cause more or less trouble in a petty way to the white settlers. The Nez Percés generally have for many years been friendly to the whites, are quite extensively engaged in agriculture, and may be considered well advanced in civilization. They show considerable interest in the education of their children, and have two schools in operation, with an attendance of 124 scholars.

Shoshones and Bannocks. — These Indians, numbering 1,037, the former 516 and the latter 521, occupy a reservation in the south-eastern part of the Territory, near Fort Hall, formerly a military post. This reservation was set apart by treaty of 1868, and executive order of July 30, 1869, and contains 1,568,000 acres. The Shoshones on this reservation have no treaty with the government. Both bands are generally quiet and peaceable, and cause but little trouble; are not disposed to engage in agriculture, and, with some assistance from the government, depend upon hunting and fishing for subsistence. There is no school in operation on the reservation.

Cœur d'Alênes, &c. — The Cœur d'Alênes, Spokanes, Kootenays, and Pend d'Oreilles, numbering about 2,000, have no treaty with the United States, but have a reservation of 256,000 acres set apart for their occupancy by executive order of June 14, 1867, lying 30 or 40 miles north of the Nez Percés reservation. They are peaceable, have no annuities, receive no assistance from the government, and are wholly self-sustaining. These Indians have never been collected upon a reservation, nor brought under the immediate supervision of an agent. So long as their country shall remain unoccupied, and not in demand for settlement by the whites, it will scarcely be desirable to make a change in their location; but the construction of the Northern Pacific Railroad, which will probably pass through or near their range, may make it expedient to concentrate them. At present they are largely under the influence of Catholic missionaries of the Cœur d'Alêne Mission.

COLORADO, NEW MEXICO, UTAH, ARIZONA, AND NEVADA.

The tribes residing in Colorado, New Mexico, Utah, Arizona, and Nevada are divided as follows: in Colorado, about 3,800; New Mexico, 19,000; Utah, 10,000; Arizona, 25,000; and Nevada, 13,000.

COLORADO.

The Indians residing in Colorado Territory are the Tabequache band of Utes, at the Los Pinos agency, numbering 3,000, and the Yampa, Grand River, and Uintah bands of the White River agency, numbering 800. They are native to the section which they now inhabit, and have a reservation of 14,784,000 acres in the western part of the Territory, set apart for their occupancy by treaty made with them in 1868. The two agencies above named are established on this reservation, the White River agency being in the northern part, on the river of that name, and the other in the south-eastern part. This reservation is much larger than is necessary for the number of Indians located within its limits; and as valuable gold and silver mines have been, or are alleged to have been, discovered in the southern part of it, the discoveries being followed by the inevitable prospecting parties and miners, Congress, by act of April 23, 1872, authorized the Secretary of the Interior to enter into negotiations with the Utes for the extinguishment of their right to the south part of it.

A few of these Indians, who have declined to remove to and remain upon the reservation, still roam in the eastern part of the Territory, frequently visiting Denver and its vicinity, and causing some annoyance to the settlers by their presence, but committing no acts of violence or extensive depredations. The Indians of Colorado have thus far shown but little interest in the pursuits of civilized life or in the education of their children. A school is in operation at the Northern or White River agency, with an attendance of forty scholars. Steps are also being taken to open one at the Southern or Los Pinos agency.

NEW MEXICO.

The tribes residing and roaming within the limits of New Mexico are the Navajoes; the Mescalero, Gila, and Jicarilla bands of Apaches; the Muache, Capote, and Weeminuche bands of Utes; and the Pueblos.

Navajoes. — The Navajoes now number 9,114, an increase of 880 over last year's enumeration. Superintendent Pope considers this increase to be mainly due to the return, during the year, of a number who had been held in captivity by the Mexicans. They have a reservation of 3,328,000 acres in the north-western part of New Mexico and north-eastern part of Arizona, set apart for them by treaty of 1868. These Indians are natives of the section of the country where they are now located. Prior to 1864 no less than seven treaties had been made with these tribes, which were successively broken on their part, and that, with but one exception, before the Senate could take action on the question of their ratification. In 1864 the Navajoes were made captives by the military, and taken to the Bosque Redondo reservation, which had been set apart for the Mescalero Apaches, where they were for a time held as prisoners of war, and then turned over to this department. After the treaty of 1868 had been concluded, they were removed to their present location, where they have, as a tribe, remained quiet and peaceable, many of them being engaged in agriculture, and in raising sheep and goats. Of these they have large flocks, numbering 130,000 head, which supply them not only with subsistence, but also with material from which they manufacture the celebrated, and for warmth and durability unequalled, Navajo blanket. They also have a stock of 10,000 horses. These Indians are industrious, attend faithfully to their crops, and even put in a second crop when the first, as frequently happens, is destroyed by drought or frost.

One school is in operation on the reservation, with an attendance of forty scholars.

Mescalero Apaches.— These Indians, numbering about 830, are at present located — not, however, upon a defined reservation secured to them — near Fort Stanton, in the eastern part of the Territory, and range generally south of that point. Prior to 1864, they were located on the Bosque Redondo reservation, where they were quiet and peaceable until the Navajoes were removed to that place. Being unable to live in harmony with the new-comers, they fled from the reservation, and until quite recently have been more or less hostile. They are now living at peace with the whites, and conducting themselves measurably well. They have no schools, care nothing apparently about the education of their children, and are not to any noticeable extent engaged in farming or in any pursuit of an industrial character. These Indians have no treaty with the United States; nor do they receive any annuities. They are, however, subsisted in part by the government, and are supplied with a limited quantity of clothing when necessary. In addition to the Mescaleros proper, Agent Curtis reports as being embraced in his agency other Indians, called by him Aguas Nuevos, 440; Lipans, 350 (probably from Texas); and Southern Apaches, 310, whose proper home is no doubt upon the Tularosa reservation. These Indians, the agent remarks, came from the Comanche country to his agency at various dates during the past year.

Gila (sometimes called Southern) Apaches.— This tribe is composed of two bands, the Mimbres and Mogollons, and number about 1,200. They are warlike, and have for years been generally unfriendly to the government. The citizens of Southern New Mexico, having long suffered from their depredatory acts, loudly demanded that they be removed; and to comply with the wish of the people, as well as to prevent serious difficulties and possibly war, it was a year or two since decided to provide the Indians with a reservation distant from their old home, and there establish them. With a view to that end a considerable number of them were collected early last year at

Cañada Alamosa. Subsequently, by executive order dated Nov. 9, 1871, a reservation was set apart for them with other roving bands of Apaches in the Tularosa Valley, to which place four hundred and fifty of them are reported to have been removed during the present year by United States troops. These Indians, although removed against their will, were at first pleased with the change, but, after a short experience of their new home, became dissatisfied; and no small portion left the reservation to roam outside, disregarding the system of passes established. They bitterly object to the location as unhealthy, the climate being severe and the water bad. There is undoubtedly much truth in these complaints. They ask to be taken back to Cañada Alamosa, their old home, promising there to be peaceable and quiet. Of course nothing can be said of them favorable to the interests of education and labor. Such of these Indians as remain on the reservation are being fed by the government. They have no treaty with the United States; nor do they receive annuities of any kind.

Jicarilla Apaches. — These Indians, numbering about 850, have for several years been located with the Muache Utes, about 650 in number, at the Cimarron agency, upon what is called "Maxwell's Grant," in North-eastern New Mexico. They have no treaty relations with the government; nor have they any reservation set apart for them. Efforts were made some years ago to have them, with the Utes referred to, remove to the large Ute reservation in Colorado, but without success. The Cimarron agency, however, has lately been discontinued; and these Apaches will, if it can be effected without actual conflict, be removed to the Mescalero agency at Fort Stanton. Four hundred Jicarilla Apaches are also reported as being at the Tierra Amarilla agency.

Muache, Weeminuche, and Capote Utes. — These bands — the Muache band, numbering about 650, heretofore at the Cimarron agency, and the other two bands, numbering 870, at the Abiquiu agency — are all parties to the treaty made with the several bands of Utes in 1868. It has been desired to have these Indians remove to their proper reservation in Colorado; but all efforts to this end have thus far proved futile. The discontinuance of the Cimarron agency may have the effect to cause the Muaches to remove either to that reservation or to the Abiquiu agency, now located at Tierra Amarilla, in the north-western part of the Territory. These three bands have generally been peaceable, and friendly to the whites. Recently, however, some of them have shown a disposition to be troublesome; but no serious difficulty is apprehended. None of them appear disposed to work for a subsistence, preferring to live by the chase and on the bounty of the government; nor do they show any inclination or desire to have their children educated, and taught the habits and customs of civilized life. Declining to remove to and locate permanently upon the reservation set apart for the Utes in Colorado, they receive no annuities, and participate in none of the benefits provided in the treaties of 1863 and 1868 with the several bands of Ute Indians referred to under the head of "Colorado."

Pueblos. — The Pueblos, so named because they live in villages, number 7,683. They have 439,664 acres of land confirmed to them by act of Congress of Dec. 22, 1858, the same consisting of approved claims under old Spanish grants. They have no treaty with the United States, and receive but little aid from the government. During the past two years efforts have been made, and are still being continued, to secure the establishment of schools in all the villages of the Pueblos, for the instruction of their children in the English language. Five such schools are now being conducted for their benefit.

The history of the Pueblos is an interesting one. They are the remains of a once powerful people, and in habits and modes of life are still clearly distinguished from all other aborigines of the continent. The Spanish invaders found them living generally in towns and cities. They are so described by Spanish historians as far back as 1540. They early revolted, though without success, against Spanish rule; and in the struggle many of their towns were burned, and much loss of life and property occasioned. It would seem, however, that, in addition to the villagers, there were others at that time living dispersed, whose reduction to Pueblos was determined upon and made the subject of a decree by Charles V. of Spain, in 1546, in order chiefly, as declared, to their being instructed in the Catholic faith. Under the Spanish government, schools were established at the villages; the Christian religion was introduced, and impressed upon the people, and the rights of property thoroughly protected. By all these means a high degree of civilization was secured, which was maintained until after the establishment of Mexican independence; when, from want of government care and support, decay followed; and the Pueblos measurably deteriorated, down to the time when the authority of the United States was extended over that country: still they are a remarkable people, noted for their sobriety, industry, and docility. They have few wants, and are simple in their habits, and moral in their lives. They are, indeed, scarcely to be considered Indians in the sense traditionally attached to that word, and, but for their residence upon reservations patented to these bands in confirmation of ancient Spanish grants, and their continued tribal organization, might be regarded as a part of the ordinary population of the country. There are now nineteen villages of these Indians in New Mexico. Each village has a distinct and organized government, with its governor and other officers, all of whom are elected annually by the people, except the *cacique*, a sort of high priest, who holds his office during life. Though nominally Catholics in religion, it is thought that their real beliefs are those of their ancestors in the days of Montezuma.

UTAH.

The tribes residing wholly or in part within the limits of Utah are the North-western, Western, and Goship bands of Shoshones; the Weber, Yampa, Elk Mountain, and Uintah bands of Utes; the Timpanagos, the San Pitches, the Pah-Vents, the Piedes, and She-be-rechers, — all, with the exception of the Shoshones, speaking the Ute language, and being native to the country inhabited by them.

North-western, Western, and Goship Shoshones. — These three bands of Shoshones, numbering together about 3,000, have treaties made with the government in 1863. No reservations were provided to be set apart for them by the terms of said treaties, the only provision for their benefit being the agreement on the part of the United States to furnish them with articles, to a limited extent and for a limited term, suitable to their wants as hunters or herdsmen. Having no reservations, but little can be done for their advancement. They live in North-western Utah and North-eastern Nevada, and are generally inclined to be industrious, many of them gaining a livelihood by working for the white settlers, while others cultivate small tracts of land on their own account.

The Weber Utes, numbering about 300, live in the vicinity of Salt Lake City, and subsist by hunting, fishing, and begging. The Timpanagos, numbering about 500, live south of Salt Lake City, and live by hunting and fishing. The San Pitches, numbering about 300, live, with the exception of some who have gone to the Uintah Valley reservation, in the country south and east of the Timpanagos, and subsist by hunting and fishing. The Pah-Vents number about 1,200, and occupy the territory south of the Goships, cultivate small patches of ground, but live principally by hunting and fishing. The Yampa Utes, Piedes, Pi-Utes, Elk Mountain Utes, and She-berechers live in the eastern and southern parts of the Territory. They number, as nearly as can be estimated, 5,200; do not cultivate the soil, but subsist by hunting and fishing, and at times by depredating in a small way upon the white settlers. They are warlike and migratory in their habits, carrying on a petty warfare pretty much all the time with the southern Indians. These bands of Utes have no treaties with the United States: they receive no annuities, and but very little assistance from the government.

The Uintah Utes, numbering 800, are now residing upon a reservation of 2,039,040 acres in Uintah Valley, in the north-eastern corner of the Territory, set apart for the occupancy of the Indians in Utah by executive order of Oct. 3, 1861, and by act of Congress of May 5, 1864. This reservation comprises some of the best farming land in Utah, and is of sufficient extent to maintain all the Indians in the Territory. Some of the Indians located here show a disposition to engage in agriculture, though most of them still prefer the chase to labor. No steps have yet been taken to open a school on the reservation. The Uintah Utes have no treaty with the United States; but an appropriation averaging about $10,000 has been annually made for their civilization and improvement since 1863.

ARIZONA.

The tribes residing in the Territory of Arizona are the Pimas and Maricopas, Papagoes, Mohaves, Moquis, and Orivas Pueblos, Yumas, Yavapais, Hualapais, and different bands of the Apaches. All are native to the districts occupied by them, respectively.

Pimas and Maricopas. — These, said to have

been in former years "Village" or "Pueblo" Indians, number 4,342, and occupy a reservation of 64,000 acres, set apart for them under the act of Feb. 28, 1859, and located in the central part of the Territory, on the Gila River. They are, and always have been peaceful, and loyal to the government; are considerably advanced, according to a rude form of civilization, and being industrious, and engaged quite successfully, whenever the conditions of soil and climate are favorable, in farming operations, are nearly self-sustaining. The relations of these bands with the neighboring whites are, however, very unfavorable to their interests; and the condition of affairs is fast growing worse. The difficulty arises out of the fact of the use, and probably the improvident use, by the whites above them, of the water of the Gila River, by which they are deprived of all means of irrigating their lands. Much dissatisfaction is manifested on this account; and the result is, so far, that many of the Indians have left the reservation, and gone to Salt River Valley, where they are making a living by tilling the soil, not, however, without getting into trouble at this point also with the settlers.

The Pimas and Maricopas are greatly interested

in the education of their children. Two schools are in operation on the reservation, with an attendance of 105 scholars. These tribes have no treaty with the United States, and receive but little assistance from the government.

Papagoes.—These Indians, numbering about 5,000, are of the same class, in some respects, as the Pueblos in New Mexico, living in villages, cultivating the soil, and raising stock for a support. They have no reservation set apart for their occupancy, but inhabit the south-eastern part of the Territory. Many of them have embraced Christianity; and they are generally well behaved, quiet, and peaceable. They manifest a strong desire to have their children educated; and steps to this end have been taken by the department. These Indians have no treaty relations with the United States, and receive no assistance from the government. The expediency of assigning to the Papagoes a reservation, and concentrating them where they can be brought within the direct care and control of the government, is under consideration by the department. There seems to be no reason to doubt that, if so established, and once supplied with implements and stock, they would become in a short time not only self-sustaining, but prosperous.

Mohaves. — These Indians have a reservation of 75,000 acres, located on the Colorado River, and set apart for them and other tribes in the vicinity of said river, under the act of March 3, 1865. The Mohaves number about 4,000, of whom only 828 are on the reservation, the rest either roaming at large or being fed at other reservations in the Territory. An irrigating canal has been built for them at great expense; but farming operations have not as yet proved very successful. Over 1,100 acres, however, are being cultivated by the Indians. The crops consist of corn, melons, and pumpkins. These Indians show but little progress in civilization. The parents objecting to the education of their children, no schools have been put in operation on the reservation, as they could be conducted only on a compulsory system. The Mohaves have no treaty stipulations with the United States; but they are partly subsisted, and are largely assisted in their farming operations, from the general incidental fund of the territory.

Yumas. — These Indians number probably 2,000. They inhabit the country near the mouth of the Colorado River, but belong to the reservation occupied by the Mohaves. They refuse, however, to remove to the reservation, and gain a scanty subsistence by planting, and by cutting wood for steamers plying on the river. Many of them remain about Arizona City, performing menial services for the whites, and gratifying their inveterate passion for gambling. They have no treaty with the United States, and receive but little assistance from the government.

Hualapais. — These Indians, numbering about 1,500, inhabit the country near the Colorado River, north of the Mohaves, ranging a considerable distance into the interior. They have been, and still are, more or less hostile, Those who are quiet and peaceable are, with members of other bands of Indians, being fed by the government at Camps McDowell, Beal's Spring, and Date Creek.

Yavapais and Apaches. — These Indians are estimated to number from 8,000 to 12,000, the lower estimate being the more reasonable. Their ranging grounds are in the central, northern, and eastern parts of the Territory. Most of them have long been hostile to the government, committing numerous robberies and murders. Earnest efforts have been made during the past year to settle them on reservations, three of which, viz., Camp Apache, Camp Grant, and Camp Verde, were set apart for their occupancy by executive order dated Nov. 9, 1871. These efforts, however, have not resulted very successfully; the Indians occasionally coming upon the reservations in large numbers, but leaving without permission, and, indeed, defiantly, whenever so disposed, oftentimes renewing their depredations before their supplies of government rations are exhausted. Many of the bands of this tribe (if it can be called a tribe; habits, physical structure, and language all pointing to a great diversity in origin among the several bands) are seemingly incorrigible, and will hardly be brought to cease their depredations and massacres except by the application of military force.

NEVADA.

The tribes residing in Nevada are Pah-Utes, Pi-Utes, Washoes, Shoshones, and Bannocks, and are native to the districts inhabited by them respectively.

Pah-Utes. — These Indians, numbering about 6,000, inhabit the western part of the State. Two reservations have been set apart for them, — one known as the Walker River, the other as the Pyramid Lake reservation, containing each 320,000 acres. These Indians are quiet, and friendly to the whites, are very poor, and live chiefly upon fish, game, seeds, and nuts, with such assistance as the government from time to time renders them. They show considerable disposition to labor; and those on the reservations, especially the Walker River reservation, are cultivating small patches of ground. The Pyramid Lake reservation affords, in addition, excellent fishing, and the surrounding settlements a ready market for the catch over and above what the Indians require for their own consumption.

No schools have been established for these Indians. They have no treaty relations with the government, and receive no annuities.

Pi-Utes. — The Pi-Utes, numbering probably 2,500, inhabit the south-eastern part of the State. They have no reservation set apart for them; nor have they any treaty with the United States. They roam about at will, are very destitute, and obtain a living principally by pilfering from the whites, although a few of them are engaged in a small way in farming. But very little can be done for these Indians by the government in their present unsettled condition. They should be brought upon one of the reservations set apart for the Indians in Nevada, or upon the Uintah reservation in Utah, where they could receive suitable care, and proper instruction in the arts of civilized life.

Washoes. — These Indians, numbering about 500, are a poor, miserable, and debauched people, and spend most of their time among the white settlements, where they gain some supplies of food and clothing by menial services. They have no reservation and no treaty, are not in charge of any agent of the government; and vice and disease are rapidly carrying them away.

Shoshones. — The Shoshones are a portion of the North-western, Western, and Goship bands, referred to under the head of "Utah." Those roaming or residing in the eastern part of Nevada number about 2,000. The remarks made respecting their brethren in Utah will equally apply to them.

Bannocks.—The Bannocks, roaming in the north-eastern part of the State, number, probably, 1,500, and are doubtless a portion of the people of that name ranging in Eastern Oregon and Southern Idaho. They have no treaty with the government, nor any reservation set apart for them, and are not in charge of any United States agent. They should, if possible, be located upon the Fort

Hall reservation in Idaho, where some steps could be taken to advance them in civilization.

THE PACIFIC SLOPE.

The Indians on the Pacific slope are divided as follows: in Washington Territory, about 14,000; in Oregon, 12,000; in California, 22,000.

WASHINGTON TERRITORY.

The tribes residing in Washington Territory are the Nisqually, Puyallup, and other confederate tribes; the D'Wamish and other allied bands; the Makahs, the S'Klallams, the Qui-nai-elts and Quileh-utes, the Yakamas, the Chehalis and other allied tribes, and the Colville, Spokanes, Cœur d'Alênes, Okanagans, and others.

Nisqually, Puyallup, and others. — These Indians, numbering about 1,200, have three reservations, containing, as per treaty of 1854, 26,776 acres, situated on the Nisqually and Puyallup Rivers, and on an island in Puget Sound. Some of these Indians are engaged in farming, and raise considerable wheat, also potatoes and other vegetables. Many are employed by the farmers in their vicinity; while others still are idle and shiftless, spending their time wandering from place to place. One school is in operation on the Puyallup reservation, with an attendance of eleven scholars.

D'Wamish and others. — The D'Wamish and other allied tribes number 3,600, and have five reservations, containing in all 41,716 acres, set apart by treaty made with them in 1855, and located at as many points on Puget Sound. Many of these Indians, particularly those residing on the Lummi reservation, are industrious farmers, raising all the produce necessary for their support, and owning a large number of cattle, horses, hogs, &c.; while others are either employed by the neighboring white farmers, or engaged in lumbering on their own account. They are generally Christianized, most of them members of the Catholic Church. One school, with 57 scholars, is in operation on the Tulalip reservation, where all the government buildings are located. This school has had a remarkable degree of success, as reported by the agent and by disinterested visitors.

Makahs. — These Indians number 604, and have a reservation of 12,800 acres, set apart by treaty made with them in 1855, and located at the extreme north-west corner of the Territory. They are a bold, hardy race, not inclined to till the soil for a support, but depending principally upon fishing and the taking of fur-seal for their livelihood. One school is in operation among them, with an attendance of 16 scholars.

S'Klallams. — These Indians, numbering 919, have a reservation of 4,000 acres, set apart by treaty made with them in 1855, and located on what is known as "Hood's Canal." Some of them are engaged, in a small way, in farming; and others are employed in logging for the neighboring saw-mills. Their condition generally is such that their advancement in civilization must necessarily be slow. A school has been established on the reservation, and is attended by 22 scholars.

Qui-nai-elts, Qui-leh-utes, Hohs, and Quits. — These Indians number 520, and have a reservation of 25,600 acres, in the extreme eastern part of the Territory, and almost wholly isolated from white settlements, set apart under a treaty made with them July 1, 1855. But one of the four tribes mentioned, the Qui-nai-elts, live upon the reservation: the others reside at different points along the coast, northward from the reservation. These declare that they never agreed to sell their country, and that they never knowingly signed any treaty disposing of their right to it. The bottom land on the reservation is heavily timbered, and a great deal of labor is required to clear it; but when cleared, it produces good crops. Many of the Indians, though in the main fish-eaters (the Qui-nai-elt River furnishing them with salmon in great abundance), are cultivating small patches, and raise sufficient vegetables for their own use. One school is in operation on the reservation, with an attendance of 15 scholars.

Yakamas. — The Yakamas number 3,000, and have a reservation in the southern part of the Territory, containing 783,360 acres, set apart for them by treaty of June 9, 1855. These Indians belong to numerous bands, confederated under the title of Yakamas. Many of them, under the able management of their present agent, have become noticeably advanced in civilization, and are good farmers or skilled mechanics. The manual-labor school at the Yakama agency has been a complete success, and of incalculable benefit in imparting to the children a practical knowledge of farming and of the different mechanical arts. Their principal wealth is in horses, of which they own 12,000. The fact that the reservation for these Indians is located east of the Cascade Mountains, away from all contact with the whites, has doubtless tended, in a great measure, to make this what it is, — the model agency on the Pacific slope: though to this result the energy and devotion of Agent Wilbur have greatly contributed. Churches have been built on the reservation, which are well attended, the services being conducted by native preachers. There are at present two schools, with an attendance of 44 scholars.

Chehalis and others, remnants of tribes, and parties to no treaty with the government. — These Indians number about 600, and have a reservation of 4,322 acres in the eastern part of the Territory, set apart for them by executive order of July 8, 1864. A considerable portion of the land in this reservation is excellent for agricultural purposes; and quite extensive crops are being raised by the Indians of the Chehalis tribe. None of the other tribes for whom the reservation was intended reside upon it, declining to do so for the reason that they do not recognize it as their own, and fear to prejudice their claims to other lands by so doing.

All these Indians have horses and cattle in abundance. They are industrious; and, being good field-hands, those of them who do not farm on their own account find ready employment from the surrounding farmers, their services always commanding the highest wages. Having no treaty relations with the government, no direct appropriations are made for their benefit. They, however, receive some assistance from the general incidental fund of the Territory. The Indians herein referred to as not living upon the reservation are of the Cowlitz, Chinook, Shoalwater Bay, and Humboldt tribes. They profess to desire a home at the mouth of the Humboldt and Coinoose Rivers, where they originated.

Colville and other Tribes. — These Indians, numbering 3,349, occupy the north-eastern portion of the Territory. They have no treaty relations with the government, and, until the present year, have had no reservation set apart for them. They are now, however, to be established, under an order of the President of July 2, 1872, in the general section of the Territory where they now are, upon a tract which is bounded on the south and east by the Columbia River, on the west by the Okinakane River, and on the north by British Columbia. The tribes for whom this reservation is designed are known as Colvilles, Okinakanes, San Poels, Lake Spokanes, Cœur d'Alênes, Calispells, and Methows. Some of these Indians, however, have settled upon valuable tracts of land, and have made extensive improvements, while others, to a considerable number, have begun farming in a small way at various points within the district from which is proposed to remove their respective tribes. It is doubtful whether these individuals will voluntarily remove to the reservation referred to, which is some distance west of their present location. It is proposed, therefore, to allow such as are engaged in farming to remain where they are, if they so desire. Owing to the influx of whites into the country thus claimed or occupied by these Indians, many of them have been crowded out; and some of them have had their own unquestionable improvements forcibly wrested from them. This for a time during the past summer caused considerable trouble, and serious difficulties were apprehended; but thus far peace has been preserved by a liberal distribution among them of agricultural implements, seeds, blankets, &c. No funds are appropriated specially for these Indians, such supplies and presents as are given them being furnished from the general incidental fund of the Territory.

OREGON.

The tribes residing in Oregon are the Umatillas, Cayuses, Walla-Wallas, Wascoes, Molels, Chasta

Scotans, Coosas, Alseas, Klamath, Modocs, and Wal-pah-pee Snakes, besides numerous other small bands. They are all native to the country. On account of the great number of small tribes and bands in this State, — the number of tribes and bands parties to the same treaty being in some cases as high as ten or fifteen, — these Indians will be treated of, and the remarks concerning them will be made, under the heads of the agencies at which they are respectively located.

Umatilla Agency. — The tribes located at this agency are the Umatillas, Cayuses, and a portion of the Walla-Wallas, and number 837. They have a reservation of 512,000 acres, situated in the north-eastern part of the State, set apart for them by treaty of June 9, 1855. This reservation is very fertile, and, as usual in such cases, has attracted the cupidity of the whites. A proposition was made last year, under the authority of Congress, to have the Indians take land in severalty, or sell and remove to some other reservation. The Indians, however, in the exercise of their treaty rights, refused to accede to this proposition. These Indians are successfully engaged in agricultural operations, are nearly self-supporting, and may be considered, comparatively speaking, wealthy. It is gratifying to state that the introduction of whiskey by whites upon this reservation, and its sale to the Indians, has, during the last year, received a decided check through the vigilance of Agent Cornoyer in causing the arrest and trial of four citizens for a violation of the law in this respect. All the parties charged were convicted, and are now in prison. This is especially worthy of note, from the fact that it is always exceedingly difficult to obtain convictions for such dealing with Indians in any section of the country. There is one school in operation on the reservation, with an attendance of twenty-seven scholars.

Warm-Spring Agency. — The Indians at this agency, known as the "Confederated Tribes and Bands of Indians in Middle Oregon," comprise seven bands of the Walla-Walla and Wasco tribes, numbering six hundred and twenty-six. They have a reservation of 1,024,000 acres, located in the central part of the State, set apart for them by the treaty of June 25, 1855. Though there is but little really good land in this reservation, many of the Indians, by reason of their industry, have succeeded measurably in their farming operations, and may be considered as self-sustaining. In morals they have greatly improved; so that polygamy, the buying and selling of wives, gambling, and drunkenness have ceased to be common among them, as in the past. There are some, however, who are disposed to wander off the reservation, and lead a vagabond life. But little advancement has been made in education among these Indians. One school is in operation at the agency, with an attendance of fifty-one scholars.

Grand-Ronde Agency. — The Indians at this agency comprise the Molalla, Clackama, Calapooia, Molel, Umpqua, Rogue River, and other bands, seventeen in all, with a total population of eight hundred and seventy. The reservation upon which these bands are located is in the north-western part of the State. It contains 69,-120 acres, and was set apart for their occupation by treaty of Jan. 22, 1855, with the Molallas, Clackamas, &c., and by executive order of June 30, 1857. Some portions of this reservation are well adapted to grain-raising, though much of it is rough and heavily timbered. An allotment of land in severalty has been directed to be made, much to the gratification and encouragement of the tribes. These Indians are inclined to industry, and show commendable zeal in cultivating their farms, growing crops which compare favororably with those of their white neighbors. Their customs and habits of life also exhibit a marked improvement. One school is in operation, with an attendance of fifty scholars.

Siletz Agency. — The Indians at this agency are the Chasta Scotons, and fragments of fourteen other bands, called, generally, Coast-tribes, numbering altogether about 2,500. These Indians, including those at the Alsea sub-agency, have a reservation of 1,100,800 acres set apart for them by treaty of Aug. 11, 1855; which treaty, however, has never been ratified, although the reservation is occupied by the Indians. They were for a long time much averse to labor for a support; but recently they have shown more disposition to follow agriculture, although traditionally accustomed to rely chiefly upon fish for food. Many already have their farms well fenced and stocked, with good, comfortable dwellings and out-houses erected thereon. There is no reason why they should not, in time, become a thoroughly prosperous people. The failure to make allotments of land in severalty, for which surveys were commenced in 1871, has been a source of much uneasiness to the Indians, and has tended to weaken their confidence in the good intentions of the government. One school is in operation on the reservation, with an attendance of twenty scholars. None of the tribes or bands at this agency have any treaty relations with the United States, unless it may be a few members of the Rogue-River band, referred to under the head of the Grand-Ronde agency.

Alsea Sub-agency. — The Indians at this sub-agency are the Alseas, Coosas, Sinselans, and a band of Umpquas, numbering in all three hundred, located within the limits of the reservation referred to under the head of the Siletz agency. The remarks made about the Indians at the Siletz agency will generally apply to the Indians of this sub-agency. The Coosas, Sinselans, and Umpquas are making considerable advancement in agriculture, and, had they advantages of instruction, would rapidly acquire a proficiency in the simpler mechanical branches of industry. The Alseas are not so tractable, and exhibit but little desire for improvement. All the assistance they receive from the government is supplied out of the limited amount appropriated for the general incidental expenses of the service in Oregon.

Klamath Agency. — The Indians belonging to this agency are the Klamaths and Modocs, and the Yahooskin and Wal-pah-pee bands of Snakes, numbering altogether about 4,000, of whom only 1,018 are reported at the agency. They have a reservation containing 768,000 acres, set apart for them by the treaty of Oct. 14, 1864, and by executive order of March 14, 1871, situated in the extreme southern portion of the State. This reservation is not well adapted to agriculture. The climate is cold and uncertain; and the crops are consequently liable to be destroyed by frosts. It is, however, a good grazing country. Although this reservation is, comparatively speaking, a new one, the Indians located upon it are making commendable progress, both in farming operations and in lumbering. A part of the Modocs, who belong by treaty to this agency, and who were at one time located upon the reservation, have, on account of their troubles with the Klamaths, — due principally to the overbearing disposition of the latter, — left the agency, and refuse to return to it. They desire to locate upon a small reservation by themselves. Under the circumstances, they should be permitted to do this, or else be allowed to select a tract on the Malheur reservation. There is no school at present in operation for these Indians.

Malheur Reservation.—This reservation, set apart by executive order of Sept. 12, 1872, is situated in the south-eastern part of the State. Upon this it is the intention of the department eventually to locate all the roving and straggling bands in Eastern and South-eastern Oregon, which can be induced to settle there. As no funds are at the disposal of the department with which to make the necessary improvements, and to provide temporary subsistence for Indians removed, the work has not yet been fairly commenced. The Indians who should be collected upon this reservation are now a constant source of annoyance to the white settlers. They hang about the settlements and military posts, begging and stealing; and, unless some prompt measures be taken to bring them under the care and control of an agent of the government, serious trouble may result at any time. Congress should make the necessary appropriation during the coming session to maintain an agent for these Indians, to erect the agency buildings, and to provide subsistence for such as may be collected and may remain upon the reservation.

Indians not upon Reservations. — There are a number of Indians, probably not less than 3,000, "renegades," and others of roving habits, who have no treaty relations with the government, and are not in charge of any agent. The tribal names of some of these are the Clatsops, Nestucals, Tillamooks, Nehalims, Snakes, and Nez Percés. The "renegades," such in fact and so called, roam on the Columbia River, and are of considerable annoyance to the agents at Warm Springs and Umatilla: others, the Snakes, two hundred in number, are upon the edge of the Grand-Ronde reservation. These live by hunting and fishing, and profess to desire to have lands allotted to them, and a school provided for their children. The Nez Percés, belonging in Idaho, to the estimated number of two hundred, are found in Wallowa Valley, in the eastern part of the State. They claim that they were not parties to the treaty with the Nez Percé tribe years ago; that the valley in which they live has always belonged to them; and they strenuously oppose its settlement by the whites.

CALIFORNIA.

The tribes in California are the Ukie, Pitt River, Wylackie, Concon, Redwood, Humboldt,

Hoonsolton, Miscott, Siah, Tule, Tejon, Coahuila, King's River, and various other bands and tribes, including the "Mission Indians," all being native to the country.

Round-Valley Agency. — The Indians belonging to this agency are the Ukies, Concons, Pitt Rivers, Wylackies, and Redwoods, numbering in all 1,700. The number has been increased during the past year by bringing in 1,040 Indians collected in Little Lake and other valleys. A reservation containing 31,683 acres has been set apart per act of April 8, 1864, and executive order of March 30, 1870, in the western and northern part of the State, for these Indians, and for such others as may be induced to locate thereon. The lands in the reservation are very fertile; and the climate admits of a widely varied growth of crops. More produce being raised than is necessary for the subsistence of the Indians, the proceeds derived from the sale of the surplus are used in purchasing stock and work-animals, and for the further improvement of the reservation. Several of the Indians are engaged in cultivating gardens, while others work as many as twenty-five or thirty acres on their own account.

The Indians on this reservation are uniformly

quiet and peaceable, notwithstanding that they are much disturbed by the white trespassers. Suits, by direction of the department, were commenced against such trespassers, but without definite results as yet; the Attorney-General having directed the United States District Attorney to suspend proceedings. Of this reservation the Indian Department has in actual possession and under fence only about 4,000 acres; the remainder being in the possession of settlers, all clamorous for breaking up the reservation and driving the Indians out.

The Indians at this reservation have shown no especial disposition to have their children educated; and no steps were taken to that end until in the summer of 1871, when a school was commenced. There is now one school in operation, with an attendance of 110 scholars. These Indians have no treaties with the government; and such assistance as is rendered them in the shape of clothing, &c., is from the money appropriated for the general incidental expenses of the Indian service in the State.

Hoopa-Valley Agency. — The Indians belonging to this agency are the Humboldts, Hoonsoltons, Miscotts, Siahs, and several other bands, numbering seven hundred and twenty-five.

A reservation was set apart per act of April 8, 1864, for these and such other Indians in the northern part of the State as might be induced to settle thereon. This reservation is situated in the north-western part of the State, on both sides of the Trinity River, and contains 38,400 acres. As a rule, sufficient is raised on the reservation to supply the wants of the Indians. These Indians are quiet and peaceable, and are not disposed to labor on the reservation in common, but will work industriously when allowed to do so on their own individual account. One school is in operation on the reservation, with an attendance of seventy-four scholars. Having no treaty relations with the United States, and, consequently, no regular annuities appropriated for their benefit, the general incidental fund of the State is used so far as may be necessary, and so far as the amount appropriated will admit, to furnish assistance in the shape of clothing, agricultural implements, seeds, &c. Besides these, their agent has a general supervisory control of certain Klamath Indians, who live adjacent to the reservation and along the banks of the Klamath River. These formerly belonged to a reservation bearing their name, which was, years ago, abandoned in consequence of the total destruction by flood of agency buildings and improvements. They now support themselves chiefly by hunting and fishing, and by cultivating small patches in grain and vegetables.

Tule-River Farm, or Agency.—The Indians located at this point are the Tules and Manaches, numbering three hundred and seventy-four. These Indians are gradually improving, are quite proficient in all kinds of farm-work, and show a good disposition to cultivate the soil on their own account. There is one school in operation at the Tule River farm, with an attendance of thirty-seven scholars. About sixty miles from the agency reside several hundred King's-River Indians, who are in a wretched and destitute condition. They desire to be attached to the agency, and have in the past received occasional supplies of food from it.

Indians not on Reservations.—In addition to the Indians located at the three agencies named, there are probably not less than 20,000, including the Mission Indians (so called), the Coahuilas, Owen's River, and others, in the southern part of the State; and those on the Klamath, Trinity, Scott, and Salmon Rivers, in the northern part.

The Mission Indians, having been for the past century under the Catholic missions established on the California coast, are tolerably well advanced in agriculture, and compare favorably with the most highly civilized tribes of the East. The Coahuilas and others inhabiting the southeastern and eastern portions of the State, and those in the north, support themselves by working for white settlers, or by hunting, fishing, begging, and stealing, except, it may be, a few of the northern Indians, who go occasionally to the reservations and the military posts in that section for assistance in the way of food.

There are also about 4,000 Owen's-River and Manache Indians east of the Sierras, whom the settlers would gladly see removed to a reservation, and brought under the care of an agent. The department has under consideration the propriety of establishing a new reservation, upon which shall be concentrated these and numerous other Indians, in which event the Tule-River agency could advantageously be discontinued.

www.ingramcontent.com/pod-product-compliance
Lightning Source LLC
LaVergne TN
LVHW010239110826
845151LV00004B/1340
* 9 7 8 1 4 2 5 5 2 3 8 1 7 *